W9-CKT-198

Essential Histories

Ancient Israel at War
853–586 BC

Brad E Kelle

Essential Histories

Ancient Israel at War
853–586 BC

First published in Great Britain in 2007 by Osprey Publishing,
Midland House, West Way, Botley, Oxford OX2 0PH, UK
443 Park Avenue South, New York, NY 10016, USA
E-mail: info@ospreypublishing.com

© 2007 Osprey Publishing Ltd.

All rights reserved. Apart from any fair dealing for the purpose
of private study, research, criticism or review, as permitted under
the Copyright, Designs and Patents Act, 1988, no part of this
publication may be reproduced, stored in a retrieval system, or
transmitted in any form or by any means, electronic, electrical,
chemical, mechanical, optical, photocopying, recording or
otherwise, without the prior written permission of the copyright
owner. Inquiries should be addressed to the Publishers.

A CIP catalog record for this book is available from the
British Library

ISBN 978 1 84603 036 9

Page layout by Ken Vail Graphic Design, Cambridge, UK
Index by Alison Worthington
Typeset in GillSans and 1 Stone seriff
Maps by The Map Studio
Originated by United Graphic Pte Ltd, Singapore
Printed in China through Bookbuilders

07 08 09 10 11   10 9 8 7 6 5 4 3 2 1

For a catalog of all books published by Osprey Military
and Aviation please contact:

Osprey Direct, c/o Random House Distribution Center,
400 Hahn Road,
Westminster, MD 21157, USA
E-mail: info@ospreydirect.com

ALL OTHER REGIONS
Osprey Direct UK, PO Box 140,
Wellingborough, Northants, NN8 2FA, UK
E-mail: info@ospreydirect.co.uk

www.ospreypublishing.com

Dedication
For Becky, of course.

Contents

Introduction

Among the powers

In the mid-9th century BC, the ancient kingdoms of Israel and Judah – existing in the territories now referred to as "the Holy Land," Israel, or Palestine – were two of several small kingdoms subsumed under an Assyrian Empire, ruled from the banks of the Euphrates River. By the latter part of the 8th century, Assyria had destroyed the Kingdom of Israel. Little more than a century later, the Kingdom of Judah suffered a similar fate at the hands of the Babylonians. Although Judah would later regain an identity, the events of this ancient time shaped a wealth of literature and continue to influence modern thinking about the so-called "Middle East."

This book examines the major military conflicts of the kingdoms of Israel and Judah from their earliest recorded encounter with the Assyrians in 853 BC, to the final destruction of Jerusalem by the Babylonians in 586 BC. These wars can provide insights into the political developments that shaped the broader history of the Ancient Near East, and the social realities that shaped the lives of ordinary people in these ancient kingdoms.

Within the broader political history of the Ancient Near East, this period first saw the dominance of the Neo-Assyrian Empire. This empire emerged in earnest around 900, and extended its dominance westward to the Mediterranean Sea by the mid-870s.

A copy of a seal inscribed with the phrase, "Belonging to Shema' servant of Jeroboam," which dates from the 8th century BC at Megiddo. "Jeroboam" here was probably Jeroboam II, King of Israel in the first half of the 8th century. Seals were used to affix personal identification to correspondence. (akg-images/Erich Lessing)

For the next two centuries, as Assyria's fortunes waxed and waned, the Empire maintained various vassal states and annexed provinces throughout the Ancient Near East. By 605, however, a weakened Assyria gave way to the Neo-Babylonian Empire. With the help of other groups like the Medes, the Babylonians assumed control of virtually all territories from the Euphrates River to the Mediterranean Sea south of Anatolia (modern Turkey) and north of Egypt. This dominance would last for nearly a century until the Babylonian Empire itself gave way to the Medes and Persians in 539.

Among these empires, many smaller kingdoms played significant roles in regional and imperial politics. Egypt exerted influence at various times throughout the region. Smaller kingdoms like Phoenicia, Philistia, Ammon, Moab, Edom, Israel, and Judah also vied for power with one other and in relation to the empires. The Kingdom of Aram-Damascus, which was located to the northeast of Israel, particularly achieved dominance around the Jordan River – even dominance over Israel and Judah from 841 to 805 – but was ultimately destroyed by Assyria around 732.

Six major periods of military conflict for Israel and Judah occurred in the context of these empires and kingdoms:

1) In 853, Israel participated in a coalition led by Aram-Damascus, which opposed the Assyrians at the battle of Qarqar;
2) 843–805 was a period of sustained conflict among Israel, Judah, and Aram-Damascus as a result of the rise of Aram-Damascus during a period of Assyrian weakness;
3) From 734 to 731, war broke out between Israel and Judah when Israel entered into an alliance with Aram-Damascus and attempted to capture Jerusalem from Judah;
4) 730–720 witnessed Israel's sustained engagement in various rebellions against Assyria;
5) After the destruction of the Kingdom of Israel, the years 714–701 included two major conflicts in which Judah attempted to throw off Assyrian domination;
6) 597–586 witnessed two conflicts in which Judah rebelled against the newly formed Babylonian Empire and ultimately fell victim to provincialization.

The Bible and Israel's history

For the history of ancient Israel and Judah, the historian is in the unique position of having a widely read document that claims to present the story of these two kingdoms in a comprehensive way. That document is what Jews call the "Bible" and Christians call the "Hebrew Bible" or "Old Testament" portion of their scripture, which also contains the "New Testament." The existence of the Bible, however, presents the historian with a dilemma. On the one hand, other non-biblical or "extra-biblical" sources exist that are not as comprehensive, but are more contemporary with the events under consideration. On the other hand, the Hebrew Bible/Old Testament (HB/OT) is more comprehensive, but the question of its historical accuracy is complicated.

With regard to the extra-biblical sources, the Israelites' participation in the battle of Qarqar in 853 is the first mention of Israel in the records of the Assyrian Empire. There are no clear Assyrian, Babylonian, or Egyptian texts that give detailed evidence for Israel and Judah during the earlier periods of their presumed existence (e.g. 13th–10th centuries BC). After 853, however, there are large numbers of textual and archeological sources, yet they offer only a small amount of straightforward, particularly first-hand material concerning Israel and Judah. Archeologists have discovered, for example, some texts from ancient Israel itself that date from the 9th to the 6th centuries BC. These are not in the form of royal annals or king-lists, but rather tend to be local and occasional documents, like *ostraca* (inscribed potsherds) and seals, or Hebrew inscriptions and letters, like records of economic

The portion of the Babylonian Chronicle, a historical annal from the reign of Nebuchadrezzar II, which records the capture of Jerusalem in 597 BC. (British Museum, London)

transactions. Textual sources from neighboring cultures are more numerous, especially the surviving collections of royal inscriptions from Assyria, Babylonia, and Egypt. Assyrian royal annals and "Eponym Chronicles" (or "*limmu*-lists"), compositions that give chronological accounts of the achievements of various Assyrian kings, provide some specific references to rulers and events in Israel and Judah, as does a variety of local correspondence.

With regard to the biblical material, the HB/OT contains two overlapping accounts of Israelite and Judean history in the Assyrian and Babylonian periods: 1 Kings 16 to 2 Kings 23, and 2 Chronicles 17–35. The former is generally considered to be part of a larger work called the "Deuteronomistic History," which includes the biblical books of Joshua through to 2 Kings. A first version of this composition may have its origins in the 8th or 7th century BC, but the biblical version clearly results from various additions and editing in later centuries. The Chronicles' account apparently stems from the

4th century BC, with even later revisions. Both compilations indicate that they draw upon earlier sources such as "the Book of the Annals of the Kings of Israel/Judah,"[1] sources that have not yet been discovered.

As a result of the prominence of these biblical texts, most of the research on Israelite and Judean history has taken place within the field of study known as "modern biblical criticism." Such study can be significantly different in both its assumptions and practices from the kinds of scripture reading done in modern synagogues and churches. In this field, the HB/OT is not viewed as a unified, coherent, and inerrant divine authority, but is recognized as being a compilation of historically conditioned writings, which were constructed over long periods of time, contain multiple genres and literary conventions, and reflect the ideologies and contexts of their writers. Especially since the 1970s, historians have increasingly taken note of the literary and ideological nature of the biblical texts, namely that the Bible, like all ancient sources, contains artistic conventions, class and gender biases, and ideological programs. Additionally, the majority of the biblical narratives appear to have been written in the centuries after 586, a period long removed from the events they describe. Research in the last two decades has also frequently shown that many of the past archeological "proofs" used to support the Bible's basic story are inadequate.

In light of these developments, historians today often conclude that non-biblical texts and artefacts are the most useful, since they are more contemporary with the events they describe, and that the HB/OT must be used cautiously and only in conjunction with other sources. While the biblical texts may contain ancient oral traditions that should not be discounted, many historians draw a distinction between the historical peoples of Israel and Judah, who actually inhabited parts of the land of modern Israel and Palestine during the Iron Age, and the biblical "Israel," a literary entity whose story exists only in the pages of the Bible.

The kingdoms of Israel and Judah *c*.9th century BC

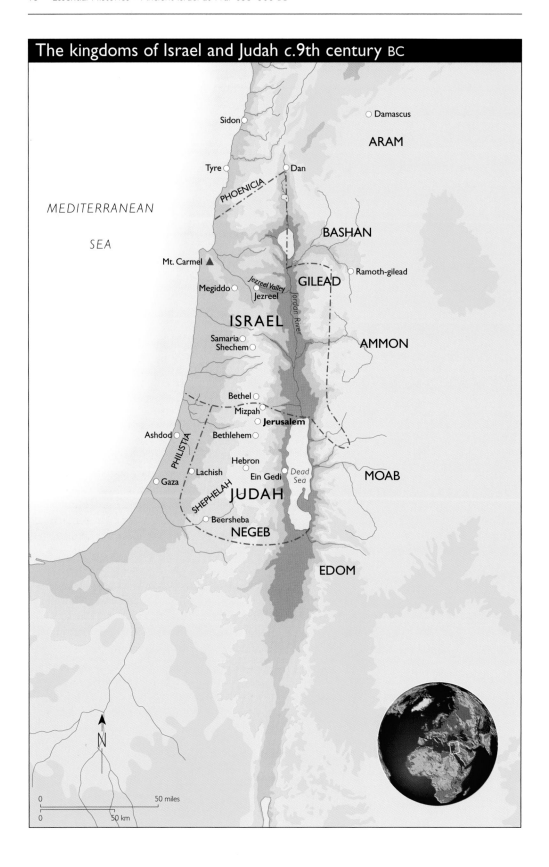

MEDITERRANEAN

SEA

Sidon○

○ Damascus

ARAM

Tyre○   ○Dan

PHOENICIA

BASHAN

Mt. Carmel ▲

○ Ramoth-gilead

GILEAD

Megiddo○   *Jezreel Valley*
            ○
            Jezreel

ISRAEL

AMMON

Samaria○
Shechem○

Bethel ○

Mizpah○

○Jerusalem

Ashdod○   Bethlehem○

PHILISTIA

Hebron
○

Lachish○   Ein Gedi○ *Dead Sea*

MOAB

Gaza○

SHEPHELAH

JUDAH

Beersheba○

NEGEB

EDOM

Jordan River

N

0   50 miles

0   50 km

The western wall ("wailing wall") of the temple mount in Jerusalem is a central place of Jewish prayer. It was once thought to be the remains of part of Solomon's temple built in the 10th century BC, but is more likely a portion of the later temple built by Herod the Great (37–4 BC). (AFP/Getty Images)

Thus, the Bible's usefulness for reconstructing the history of Israel and Judah remains debated. Should we reconstruct major conflicts from Israel's past without using the Bible? Should we give priority to non-biblical data but use the Bible as a secondary source? Or should we accept the biblical accounts as historical unless they are directly falsified? This study of Israel's wars takes the position that a middle ground course is best: all available sources, meager or contested though they may be, should be taken into account, yet each should be weighed equally, without automatically privileging or distrusting either the biblical story or non-biblical data. In the end, both the biblical and Ancient Near Eastern texts are literary constructions with theological and ideological agendas, which are often propagandistic and selective. Even though the Bible tells a detailed story, historians must still make choices concerning how to weigh different pieces of evidence on a case-by-case basis. Any conclusion based on only one source, even if it is the Bible, must remain tentative. This approach means that the historian should explain how he or she views each source used in light of its genre, purposes, origins, context, and connection with other sources. Such a combination of sources, complex though it may be, is the window into the conflicts and life of Israel and Judah among the powers of the 9th to the 6th centuries BC.

Chronology

The HB/OT, particularly 1 and 2 Kings, preserves a comprehensive chronology of kings and events in Israel and Judah. Yet these texts are a controversial chronological source, as the figures given cannot be sorted out coherently. The Bible has merged the data from the two distinct kingdoms, and the texts contain two different systems of keeping chronology. One system gives the total years of a king's reign: "[Ahaz] reigned 16 years in Jerusalem."[2] The other system synchronizes kings of Israel and Judah: "In the 17th year of Pekah son of Remaliah [of Israel], King Ahaz son of Jotham began to reign."[3] Though intertwined, these systems do not align, nor do the biblical books contain identical names for all the kings. Efforts to unravel the biblical chronology have considered the possibilities that different sources used by the biblical writers may have employed different calendar systems, that co-regencies may have existed, that other manuscripts (no longer surviving) may preserve the original figures, and that theological perspectives may have distorted the data.

Thus, in order to get even a general sense of the chronology for the kingdoms of Israel and Judah, non-biblical sources from Assyria and Babylonia must be used with the Bible. These sources record natural events like eclipses, which allow them to be dated more precisely, and are less schematic and theological than the HB/OT's chronologies. Still, despite mentions of Israelite and Judean kings in some of these sources, and mentions of Assyrian and Babylonian kings in the HB/OT, no effort has arrived at an agreed chronology, and proposals can vary as much as a decade for the dates of a particular event. One can offer relatively secure dates for some particular periods, but not a comprehensive chronology.

909 Adad-nirari II founds the Neo-Assyrian Empire

875 Ashurnasirpal II collects tribute from cities in Syria-Palestine

853 Ahab of Israel and coalition partners battle Shalmaneser III at Qarqar; Ahab dies shortly after

849–845 Continued coalition battles with Shalmaneser III

843 Hazael usurps throne in Aram-Damascus and begins hostilities with Israel

841 Jehu seizes throne in Israel and pays tribute to Shalmaneser III

838–805 Assyria in decline; Hazael dominates Israel and surrounding kingdoms

810 Adad-nirari III leads Assyrian resurgence to the west

805–803 Israel throws off Aram-Damascus; Adad-nirari III captures Damascus; Joash of Israel pays tribute to Assyria

802 Joash ends Amaziah of Judah's bid for independence from Israel

788–750 Period of restoration and prosperity in Israel and Judah

773 Shalmaneser IV recaptures Damascus

773–745 Internal revolts in Assyria and loss of Assyrian presence in the west

750 Rezin becomes king in Aram-Damascus and invades Israelite territory; Pekah emerges as pro-Aramean rival claimant in Israel

747–730 Piankhy of Ethiopia occupies Egyptian Delta

745 Tiglath-pileser III takes Assyrian throne and begins westward campaigns

740–738 Menahem of Israel pays tribute to Tiglath-pileser III

734 Pekah seizes throne in Israel and joins an anti-Assyrian coalition led by Rezin

734–733 Rezin and Pekah besiege Ahaz in Jerusalem

733   Ahaz of Judah pays tribute to
        Tiglath-pileser III

733–731 Tiglath-pileser III defeats Rezin and
        allies and annexes territories in Galilee
        and Transjordan; Hoshea overthrows
        Pekah in Israel

731   Hoshea sends tribute to Tiglath-pileser III

730   Accession of Osorkon IV in Egypt

729   Tiglath-pileser III captures Babylon

728–727 Renewed rebellion in west;
        Tiglath-pileser III dies on campaign;
        Hoshea rebels then submits to
        Shalmaneser V of Assyria

727–725 Israel joins rebellion led by Tyre
        and appeals for help to "King So" of
        Egypt; Shalmaneser V provincializes
        Samaria and besieges Tyre

724–722 Israel joins renewed western
        rebellion; Shalmaneser V besieges
        Samaria for three years and captures it

722–721 Rebellion across Empire at
        Shalmaneser V's death

720   Sargon II suppresses revolt led by
        Yaubi'di of Hamath, recaptures Samaria,
        and exiles around 30,000 people; Assyria
        opens trade with the Egyptian Delta

715   Judean troops fight alongside Assyrians
        in Urartu

715   Shabako of Ethiopia invades Egyptian
        Delta and reverses relations
        with Assyria

714   Merodach-baladan of Babylon sends
        emissaries to Judah

714–711 Judah joins anti-Assyrian rebellion
        led by Yamani of Ashdod; Sargon II
        reclaims Babylon, provincializes Ashdod,
        and destroys some Judean territory

710   Cyprus and King Midas of Phrygia
        submit to Assyria

705   Sargon II dies on battlefield in
        Anatolia; rebellion throughout Empire

705–701 Hezekiah of Judah leads a western
        rebellion including Ekron, Sidon,
        and Ashkelon

701   Sennacherib of Assyria defeats
        Egyptians led by Taharqa at Eltekeh,
        captures 46 Judean towns, exiles
        200,150 people, and besieges
        Jerusalem; Hezekiah capitulates but
        remains in power

673   Taharqa repels Assyrian king
        Esarhaddon's invasion of Egypt

671   Esarhaddon defeats Taharqa and
        captures Memphis

669–668 Esarhaddon dies on a
        renewed campaign against
        Taharqa; Ashurbanipal continues
        the campaign; Judah contributes
        troops to Ashurbanipal

664   Ashurbanipal defeats the Ethiopians
        and captures Thebes

652–648 Rebellion in Babylon led by
        Ashurbanipal's brother

643–642 Widespread western revolt
        against Ashurbanipal

641–610 Josiah rules in Judah; Assyria in
        decline; Pharaoh Psammetichus I
        dominates Syria-Palestine

626   Nabopolassar frees Babylon
        from Assyria and founds
        Neo-Babylonian dynasty

614   Medes capture Ashur and align
        with Babylonians

612   Babylonians and Medes destroy
        Nineveh

610   Pharaoh Necho II aids Assyria against
        Babylonians at Haran and kills Josiah
        at Megiddo

609   Babylonians and Medes defeat Egyptians
        and Assyrians at Haran; Necho II makes
        Jehoiakim king in Judah

605   Babylonians defeat Egyptians at
        Carchemish; Nebuchadrezzar claims
        throne of Babylon; Judah becomes
        Babylonian vassal

601–600 Necho II halts Nebuchadrezzar's
        invasion of Egypt and moves into
        Gaza; Jehoiakim withholds tribute
        from Babylon

597   Nebuchadrezzar captures Jerusalem
        and enthrones Zedekiah

595–4 Elam leads rebellion in east

592–591 Pharaoh Psammetichus II visits
        Judah and Phoenicia; Zedekiah
        withholds tribute from Babylon

588–587 Nebuchadrezzar besieges
        Jerusalem and repels army of Pharaoh
        Apries (Hophra)

586   Babylonians destroy Jerusalem and
        its temple

The rise of the kingdoms

The centuries of conflict covered in this volume saw ancient Israel and Judah engaged with allies and enemies from four primary areas – Assyria, Aram-Damascus, Babylonia, and Egypt – in a territory now called the Ancient Near East or Fertile Crescent. This area stretched from the Persian Gulf, up the Tigris and Euphrates rivers, below the Zagros mountains, to the eastern coast of the Mediterranean Sea, down to the Gulf of Aqaba, and over Gaza to the Nile River. It was a highly active trade route, whose communication avenues and political activities fostered the growth of kingdoms and empires.

The kingdoms that arose in Assyria and Babylonia became the major empires that dominated the Ancient Near East after the mid-9th century BC, and engulfed smaller kingdoms like Israel and Judah in the maelstrom of their activities. Each of the four primary areas had, however, a long history of development, which stretched back to around 2000 BC and formed the background for the

sequence of conflicts relevant to the present study. The kingdoms of Israel and Judah, apparently emerging around 1200 to 1000, were relatively late in their development. While the precise time and dynamics of their emergence remain difficult to establish, direct Israelite and Judean engagement with kingdoms from these primary areas began in the mid-9th century.

The kingdoms to the east and south

Between about 2000 BC and the outbreak of conflicts around 850, the history of the Ancient Near East was characterized by the

The great Egyptian pyramids at Giza from the Fourth Dynasty (c.2600 BC). These pyramids had already been standing for nearly a millennium and a half by the time Israel emerged on the scene in Syria-Palestine, a stark reminder of Israel's status as a relative "late-comer" to the stage of world history. (akg-images)

The Ancient Near East c.9th century BC

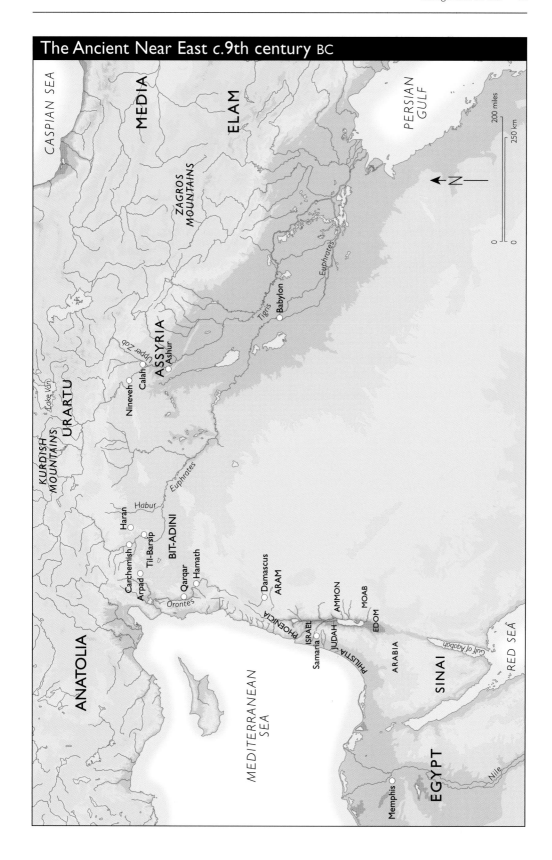

continual shifting of the center of power between Assyria, Babylonia, and Egypt, with smaller powers such as the Arameans (in Syria), the Hittites (in Anatolia), and Urartu (in eastern Asia Minor) arising occasionally. Out of this matrix of ascendancy and decline, the Kingdom of Assyria eventually arose as the dominant force in the Ancient Near East.

Assyria actually began to emerge around 3000 BC as a conglomeration of various independent city-states located between the Tigris and Euphrates rivers. In the 2000s, the area coalesced into a unified entity, and by c.1800 Shamshi-Adad I had expanded Assyrian control into central Syria. Throughout the following centuries, the "Assyrian heartland" consisted of a triangle bordered by the Kurdish mountains, the Tigris River, and the Upper Zab River, with its chief cities at Ashur, Calah, and Nineveh. Assyria's efforts at expansion, however, would later enlarge its territory to include a region that stretched from the Persian Gulf in the south to the Zagros mountains in the east, and from the Kurdish mountains in the north to the Mediterranean Sea in the west.

Throughout its history, Assyria's geographical location made it particularly vulnerable to enemies from the north and south. For instance, in the 18th century BC, the Babylonians under Hammurabi moved up the Tigris and came to rule nearly the whole of the Assyrian heartland. After Hammurabi's reign, however, Babylonia itself fell under the power of more distant kingdoms like the Kassites and Hittites. Around 1700 BC, Assyria entered a period of weakness that would last for some 400 years, when its territory was brought under the dominance of the Kingdom of Mitanni, centered on the Habur River.

At this time, the center of power in the Ancient Near East shifted back to Egypt. For over 100 years, Egypt had been ruled by the Hyksos, Semitic rulers from Asia. But around 1550 BC, the Hyksos were expelled and an Egyptian dynasty led from Thebes established an empire that would dominate the western part of the Fertile Crescent, including the land

of Canaan or "Syria-Palestine," until around 1200. This so-called "New Kingdom" took shape under pharaohs like Thutmose III, Amenhotep, and Ramesses II, and saw the Egyptian annexation of territories from Nubia in Upper Egypt to cities in northern Canaan, even as far north as the Euphrates River. While Assyria and Babylonia sent diplomatic presents to the Egyptian rulers, Egypt's major enemy was the Hittites from Anatolia. After years of battling one another to a stalemate, the Egyptians and Hittites entered into a treaty during the time of Ramesses II and effectively shared domination of the Ancient Near East.

Throughout these years, the eastern powers of Assyria and Babylonia were only able to gain strength for brief periods, and even then had to contend with nearby threats like those of Elam and Mitanni. One such moment occurred with the emergence of the Assyrian king Ashur-uballit I (1363–1328). In the midst of Egypt's western domination, he was able to control Babylonia and correspond with the Egyptian pharaoh as an equal. Although the years immediately following his reign would see the loss of control over Babylonia, this first self-proclaimed "King of Assyria" began Assyria's westward expansion toward the Mediterranean Sea, which would grow incrementally over the next several centuries.

At the beginning of the so-called "Iron Age" (c.1200), the geo-political face of the Ancient Near East shifted dramatically with the arrival of the "Sea Peoples," sea-borne groups perhaps related to Mycenaean civilization, who entered the areas of Egypt and the Mediterranean coast. This period also witnessed the collapse of the Egyptian and Hittite empires and the regression of Assyrian power. Control of Egypt splintered among different dynasties ruling from different areas, and Assyria's hegemony over Babylonia faltered under pressure from neighboring regions.

During this period a group arose that would play a prominent role in the affairs of Israel, Judah, and the entire area of Syria-Palestine over the next 500 years. The Arameans, a relatively non-unified group of Semitic people who lived in the

One of the two present-day mounds at the site of the ancient city of Nineveh, former capital of the Assyrian Empire in the 7th century BC. (Time & Life Pictures/ Getty Images)

area of the middle Euphrates, Orontes River, and southern Syria, filled the vacuum left by the collapse of the Hittite Kingdom in northern Syria. They made their first appearance in Assyrian texts after 1200 and would reappear with varying levels of political and military power until their ultimate subjugation by the Assyrians c.730.

Although the years between 1200 and 900 are the most immediate background preceding ancient Israel's major military conflicts, this period is a relative dark age in terms of available historical sources. It seems to have been characterized by the switching of power between the Assyrians, Arameans, and Egyptians. For example, the Assyrian king, Tiglath-pileser I (1114–1076), claimed to have crossed the Euphrates 28 times to fight the Arameans. After his reign, however, Assyria was unable to hold western territories against the Arameans, and the Aramean Kingdom of Bit-Adini controlled the area around the Euphrates crossing in northern Syria. The HB/OT texts, if reliable in this regard, likewise indicate that the Aramean kingdoms of Aram Zobah and Damascus gained hegemony over the territory further west and south.[4] Egypt also made an attempt at resurgence during this timeframe, when Pharaoh Sheshonq (biblical "Shishak"[5]) founded the 22nd Dynasty and attempted to reassert Egyptian control over Syria-Palestine by undertaking a military campaign northward into central Canaan and the Mediterranean coast (c.925).

The decisive shift in the political world of the Ancient Near East, a shift that would set the stage for the major military conflicts of the mid-9th to the early 6th centuries, began with the reemergence of Assyria under Ashur-dan II c.930. His reign marked the beginning of the "Neo-Assyrian Empire" that would dominate the Ancient Near East for the next three centuries, and force even the former powers of Babylonia and Egypt to struggle in its shadow. His son, Adad-nirari II, began a limited practice of annexing conquered territories, a practice that would be undertaken more systematically in the centuries that followed. The high point of Assyrian power drew near, however, when Ashurnasirpal II (883–859) subdued Assyria's major northern enemy of Urartu, gained control over the region of Bit-Adini in the west, reached the Mediterranean Sea by 875, and collected tribute from kingdoms in Syria-Palestine. These actions inaugurated some 50 years of continuous Assyrian military expansion. This expansion reached its climax under Ashurnasirpal's successor, Shalmaneser III, the king with whom Israel's major military conflicts under consideration in this volume began. He initiated the Assyrian practice of annual military

A representation of a Philistine warrior found at an Egyptian temple in Thebes. The Philistines were part of the "Sea Peoples," who moved into the area of Egypt and Syria-Palestine around 1200 BC. The typical Philistine headdress is made of horsehair or feathers. (akg-images/Erich Lessing)

campaigns and campaigned west of the Euphrates 21 times during his 35-year reign. Shalmaneser effectively established Assyrian control over the territory from Babylonia in the east, to Urartu in the north, to Syria-Palestine in the west.

In the earliest stage of dominance, the Assyrians did not enact a systematic plan for the construction of a unified empire. Shalmaneser did not annex western kingdoms into imperial provinces but made them into vassal kingdoms with a required annual tribute. Nonetheless, over the following years the Assyrians gained ever-increasing control through the development of a complex bureaucracy, provincial system, and standing army. It is precisely their efforts in this regard that provoked reactions from various kingdoms like Israel and Judah. Alliances were forged, rebellions were instigated, and capitulations were made – all in response to Assyria's attempts to control the Ancient Near Eastern world. Western resistance to Assyria began

in earnest in 853 when Shalmaneser encountered a newly formed coalition that included one of Israel's first significant kings.

The emergence of Israel and Judah

Around 1200, when the Ancient Near East plunged into 200 years of a dark age characterized by the collapse of empires and a dearth of historical sources, Israel emerged on the scene. Hence, the origin of the Israelite and Judean kingdoms is one of the most debated periods in their history. Any understanding of the events largely depends on interpretation of the relevant HB/OT texts.

The biblical texts, especially the books of Joshua and Judges (which were written many centuries after the events they describe), tell a comprehensive story. According to them, the kingdoms of Israel and Judah began as a unified people. More specifically, they consisted of 12 tribes descended from the 12 sons of Jacob, who escaped from slavery in Egypt and conquered the land of Canaan. The biblical story continues in the books of Samuel and Kings, which tell that David reigned over a unified kingdom of Israel and Judah from Jerusalem for about 30 years after the year 1000. His son, Solomon, then reigned for about 40 years and established a centralized kingdom with a national building program. Furthermore, Solomon is said to have created an empire in Syria-Palestine that spanned the area from the Euphrates River to the Mediterranean Sea to the Egyptian border.[6] According to the biblical story, it was only after the death of Solomon (c.920) that Israel and Judah split into two kingdoms with different ruling dynasties.

Historians are unsure how this biblical picture fits with historical reality between 1200 and 900. There is a growing consensus today that Israel did not conquer the land of Canaan from the outside but emerged from the consolidation of various foreign and indigenous elements. Similarly, many question whether Israel existed as a centralized kingdom in the 10th century,

One of the bronze bands from the gates at Balawat, which depicts Assyrian chariots and horsemen setting out on a campaign to Hamath in 849 BC. The Assyrian king Shalmaneser III campaigned throughout northern Syria between 853 and 845 BC.
(British Museum, London)

and thus Israel's creation of an empire in Syria-Palestine at that time. The biblical traditions themselves, for example, give varying pictures of both Israel's emergence and Solomon's power that cannot be squared with one another.[7] Evidence from outside the Bible only complicates the picture. One non-biblical inscription from the 1200s mentions Israel in passing but designates Israel only as a people (not a city or land) subdued by an Egyptian pharaoh. Archeological remains show the destruction of a few Canaanite cities and the emergence of small agricultural villages in the highlands of Syria-Palestine around 1200. But even these destroyed cities do not always concur with the biblical conquest stories, and the villages appear to continue the indigenous culture of the preceding period and do not seem to be the settlements of an outside group. Remains of monumental architecture (such as city walls or gates) that may date to Solomon's time in the 10th century have been found at some Israelite cities,[8] but pottery remains at those sites may equally suggest that the architecture comes from the following century. No extra-biblical texts mention Solomon or an empire centered in Jerusalem, and there is minimal archeological evidence of international commerce in Judean territory during this period. Also, Jerusalem itself

shows no occupational evidence of having served as the urban capital of an expansive empire during these years.

Taken as a whole, the evidence that is available suggests that Israel and Judah originated in groups of villagers who came together for religious and political purposes in the hill country of Syria-Palestine around 1200. Despite the HB/OT's picture, their early existence probably differed little from the many similar small kingdoms emerging across the area, and simply represented yet another example of a wave of settlements going on at this time. The following centuries – the biblical times of David and Solomon – probably saw the development of a minor chiefdom or city-state centered on Jerusalem, which was perhaps capable of dominating western Syria-Palestine and the northern Transjordan. By the time of the Neo-Assyrian Empire in the early 800s, however, two kingdoms clearly existed in southern Syria-Palestine: Israel with its capital at Samaria, and Judah with its capital at Jerusalem. These took their place among the many small kingdoms of the day, including coastal cities like Tyre and Sidon, the Neo-Hittite cities in Anatolia, the Aramean Kingdom in Damascus, the Ammonite, Moabite, and Edomite kingdoms to the east, and the Philistine cities to the west. Over the next four centuries, each of these civilizations would be engulfed by shifting empires from the east and south, and would allow their politics, religion, and ideology to transform them into warring sides.

The politics of religion, commerce, and war

The armies of Israel, Judah, and Aram

Four warring sides were the primary participants in the outbreak of Israel's major military conflicts in the mid-9th century BC: Israel, Judah, Aram-Damascus, and Assyria. The HB/OT provides most of the available information for the Israelite and Judean militaries in this time, along with a few references in Assyrian and Babylonian texts and evidence from archeological remains. The fullest biblical descriptions relate, however, to other periods of Israel's history, and the accuracy of all the biblical and extra-biblical descriptions remains debated.

As the HB/OT presents it, in the earliest period of a unified Israel and Judah (c.1200–1050), Israel's army was simply a militia of adult males summoned on an occasional basis. A lack of constancy and strength necessitated the avoidance of open battles and the practice of primarily guerrilla tactics, such as individual raids and night attacks.[9] By the reigns of David and Solomon (c.1050–920), the HB/OT claims the presence of a standing army that included chariots and cavalry:

> Solomon also had forty thousand stalls of horses for his chariots, and twelve thousand horsemen … as well as all of Solomon's storage cities, the cities for his chariotry, the cities for his cavalry.[10]

Both biblical and non-biblical sources confirm that standing armies were in place in Israel and Judah by the Assyrian period in the 9th century. Little is known of the specific recruitment, composition, and organization of these forces, but they consisted of three primary elements: infantry, chariotry, and cavalry. Infantry formed the primary fighting force and included spearmen, equipped with spears, lances, javelins, and shields; archers, utilizing bows of various sizes, carrying quivers on their backs, and often accompanied by separate shield-bearers; and slingers, organized in combat pairs. The infantry had units of 1,000, 100, 50, and 10, and may have lived in garrisons in key cities.[11] Biblical texts and Assyrian reliefs portray Israelite and Judean infantrymen as outfitted with shields, helmets, and coats of armor, sometimes including a scarf around the head and covering the ears.[12] While the prominence of cavalry remains unclear, chariotry was particularly important during the reigns of Omri and Ahab (879–853). Israel and Judah did not have a navy, but biblical texts suggest the periodic use of ships for commercial purposes.[13] Alongside the regular army core, royal guards served the king personally, and occasional levies could raise additional temporary troops.

Only scant references exist concerning the leadership of the Israelite and Judean military. The king was the head of the army. Offices like "captain" (Hebrew, *shalish*)[14] and "commander" (Hebrew, *sar*)[15] were important for the army and chariotry, yet the precise nature of these offices and how one achieved them remains uncertain.

The size of the forces fielded by Israel and Judah varied in different periods and conflicts. For a battle with the Assyrians in 853, for example, an Assyrian inscription credited King Ahab of Israel with 10,000 soldiers, 2,000 chariots, and no cavalry, although the number of chariots seems high here when compared with other forces. Archeological excavations at the city of Megiddo have revealed the presence of what appear to be stables, probably used for chariot forces during the time of Omri and Ahab. The stables had the capacity to hold nearly 500 horses. Second Kings 13: 7 describes Judah's army during a time of

oppression by Aram-Damascus as consisting of 10,000 soldiers, 50 cavalry, and 10 chariots, but texts reflecting other periods credit the Judean army with as many as 300,000 soldiers:

Under their command was an army of three hundred seven thousand five hundred, who could make war with mighty power, to help the king against the enemy.[16]

An Assyrian relief showing stone-slingers in action. Slingers, along with spearmen and archers, formed the core of the Assyrian infantry. (akg-images/Erich Lessing)

While there is some evidence for offensive campaigns and city sieges undertaken by Israel and Judah during the 9th to the 6th centuries, their primary military tactic was the forming of alliances with surrounding states.

Flint stones used in slingshots during the battle of Lachish in 701 BC. Such distance weapons were probably used by both the Assyrian forces besieging the city and the Judean forces defending it. (British Museum, London)

These alliances were normally attempts to resist Assyrian or Babylonian hegemony and to turn back these empires' attempted reprisals against rebellious subordinates. Thus, the military activity of Israel and Judah primarily served defensive purposes. The fortifications of major cities, including gates with strong towers and double walls connected by partitions, reflected this reality and were designed to defend against potential sieges.

When drawn out of their cities, Israelite and Judean forces practiced conventional warfare known throughout the ancient Near East, but without the well-developed machinery and elite corps of the Assyrian Empire. Israelite chariotry, and especially cavalry, were limited to a supportive role. The spearmen constituted the major fighting force at the front, with archers and slingers providing assistance from the rear.

Israelite and Judean relations with their immediate neighbors vacillated between cooperation and hostility, but the militaries of these neighbors seem to have been similar to the forces of Israel and Judah. For example,

the Kingdom of Aram-Damascus, located immediately north of Israel and east of the Jordan River, at times constituted Israel's most powerful enemy and at other times their most significant ally. Assyrian and biblical texts provide nearly all the available information concerning the military constitution and practices of Aram-Damascus, but reveal few details. The general composition of the army was infantry, chariots, and cavalry. The same Assyrian inscription that described Israel's army in 853 assigned Damascus 20,000 infantry, 1,200 chariots, and 1,200 cavalry.

Perhaps because the various Aramean kingdoms like Damascus never united into an empire, their primary military tactic, like that of Israel and Judah, was the forming of coalitions. Damascus-led coalitions were active in the area of Hamath in the late 9th century and were involved in several attempts to throw off Assyrian domination of Syria-Palestine from the mid-9th to mid-8th centuries. The references to "governors of the districts" and "commanders" that replace kings in 1 Kings 20: 14–15, 24 may also indicate an Aramean practice of organizing subdued territories into administrative districts.

The might of the Assyrian Empire

Israel, Judah, and Aram-Damascus lived in a shadow cast from the east. Assyria was a militaristic state, which organized its political, domestic, and social life around warfare. As a result, Assyria developed the most powerful fighting force in the history of the Ancient Near East prior to the emergence of Persia.

Most of the available information about the Assyrian army relates to the late 700s through to the 600s, but a standing army came into existence under Tiglath-pileser III in the mid-700s. The basic elements included the king's elite guard, infantry, chariotry, cavalry, and engineers. The infantry

A pictorial relief from the Assyrian king Tiglath-pileser III's (c.745 BC) palace in Nimrud. The relief shows an Assyrian siege-engine supported by archers during the siege of a city. The background also pictures impaled citizens or soldiers. (Werner Forman Archive)

consisted of heavy infantry (spearmen) and light infantry (archers and slingers). Visual representations show infantrymen wearing coats of mail, short tunics, leggings, and high boots.

As early as the mid-9th century, however, the cavalry and chariotry formed the elite corps of the army. Reliefs from Nineveh picture cavalrymen as working in pairs, normally barefoot, without a saddle, and using a composite bow with a long sword on their side. Assyrian chariots functioned as light artillery and often carried a driver, archer, and shield-bearer.

The army's organization was hierarchical, with the king as the head who often led campaigns in person. The "field marshal" (*tartan*) was beneath the king. The basic unit was a company of 50 men under the command of a captain. Some troops were permanent, while others were probably called up through an institutional requirement to perform military service

The remains of an Assyrian siege ramp on the southwest corner of Lachish from 701 BC. The ramp was a typical feature of Assyrian siege warfare. It served to move battering rams and troops into position against the city walls. (http://www.lmlk.com/research/lmlk_lachish-tel.htm)

each year for a set amount of time. Thus, the Assyrians could deploy forces as large as several hundred thousand soldiers. For example, Shalmaneser III records crossing the Euphrates in 845 with 120,000 men. The size of the forces varied, however, in different periods and conflicts. The standing army probably represented the nucleus, but the majority of the force was called up on special occasions. The Assyrians added more levies of troops as the campaign progressed and often incorporated whole units of conquered armies into the Assyrian forces.

The Assyrian army practiced three major tactics: open battles, city sieges, and psychological warfare. As the Empire expanded, siege warfare became the most prominent. The Assyrians surrounded a city to cut off supplies, constructed siege ramps of earth and stone, and moved large battering rams into place against the walls. Such a siege of the Judean city of Lachish appears in reliefs at the Assyrian palace in Nineveh, and the archeological remains

of a 160–190ft (50–60m) long siege ramp are still in view at the site. Sennacherib, the Assyrian king at the time, recorded his tactics:

As for Hezekiah, the Judean, I besieged 46 of his fortified walled cities... Using packed-down ramps and applying battering rams, infantry attacks by mines, breeches, and siege machines, I conquered them.[17]

The Assyrians were perhaps most feared for their tactics of deportation and brutality. When a city fell, the Assyrians regularly deported a significant portion of the population and resettled them in Assyrian cities or undeveloped parts of the Empire. In the final centuries of the Empire, the Assyrians deported perhaps as many as four to five million people. The purpose of deportation was not to punish but to enhance Assyrian economy and security. As these deportees eventually lost their ethnic identity, they created a mixed society that characterized major Assyrian cities.

Assyrian brutality toward conquered peoples was also legendary across the Empire. After the fall of a major city, Assyrians were known to burn houses, gouge out citizens' eyes, flay captives alive,

Bronze and iron arrowheads discovered in Judean ruins. Such arrowheads appear in the ruins of the ancient Judean city of Lachish, the southwestern city that was the center of a major battle between Assyrian and Judean forces in 701 BC. (British Museum, London)

pile up severed heads, and impale corpses on stakes around the city. For example, the Assyrian king Ashurnasirpal II (883–859 BC) describes Assyrian brutality toward a conquered city:

Many of the captives taken from them I burned in a fire… I cut off their hands to the wrist, from others I cut off their noses, ears, and fingers; I put out the eyes of many of the soldiers… I burnt their young men and women to death. (Saggs, *The Might That Was Assyria*, 261.)

While this brutality has been understood as indicating a bloodthirsty nature, it was not perpetrated on every city in every situation. These actions were performed against chosen targets, perhaps as psychological warfare – an attempt to convince nearby kingdoms to submit or remain loyal. Assyrian inscriptions like those of King Tiglath-pileser III often follow the description of some destruction or brutality with a comment about a neighboring kingdom: "the fame of my lordship [(and of) my heroic deeds they heard, and they made supplication to] my lordship."[18]

Once the results of war had been achieved, the Assyrians maintained control of their expansive empire primarily through treaty relationships with equals or vassals. When a kingdom submitted voluntarily to Assyria, it became a "satellite kingdom." Satellites accepted Assyrian authority and paid annual tribute, but remained relatively independent and locally governed. If a kingdom refused to submit or rebelled after initial submission, the Assyrians reduced it to a "vassal kingdom" and annual tribute was reimposed; Assyrian officials and perhaps a garrison were stationed there, but the local ruling family remained in power if they promised loyalty. When a vassal rebelled, the Assyrians incorporated it into the Empire as a "province": local rulers were removed, portions of the population deported, and an Assyrian governor placed in control. The Kingdom of Israel moved through this very sequence from 730–720. The Assyrians were reluctant, however, to provincialize Syria-Palestine's southernmost kingdoms like Judah, because they formed buffer zones with Egypt at the far southwest corner of the Empire.

Judean citizens of Lachish departing for deportation to Babylonia after the city's fall in 701 BC, as portrayed on an Assyrian relief at the royal palace in Nineveh. The Assyrians often allowed women and children deportees to travel in carts. (akg-images/Erich Lessing)

Motives for war

Political and religious ideology was a motivational factor for the warring sides in the mid-9th century and beyond. Assyrian state ideology saw the conduct of wars on behalf of the state as the king's primary role. The king was expected to lead a military campaign every year of his reign, and scribes denoted a king's years in terms of his military achievements. This ideology also had a religious aspect, as the king's obligatory campaigns were undertaken for the sake of the chief Assyrian god, Ashur. The role of religion was apparent in the presence of priests and diviners, who performed rituals before campaigns and marched out at the head of the army. Such religious convictions were also present in Israel and Judah, where the HB/OT presents their wars as the god

Yahweh's wars, and depicts kings as consulting religious personnel about military activities.[19]

Defensive motives also provided the catalyst for military campaigns. Particularly in the case of Assyria, the lack of natural boundaries around the homeland necessitated the conquering of surrounding threats. Perhaps the most significant motivations, however, were economic. Assyrian campaigns served to secure access to agricultural and commercial resources lacking in the heartland, and resources from spoil and tribute supplied major building projects. Assyrian kings sought control of trade across the Fertile Crescent, particularly of metals, timber, and horses. The territories of Israel and Judah were of particular interest to the Assyrians because they were located on the land bridge between the major centers of Mesopotamia and Egypt, and thus sat in the geographical center of the primary trade routes. As Assyrian dominance grew in this area, the loss of commercial control and the heavy economic burden of tribute fostered the seeds of resistance and rebellion among the kingdoms of the west.

The emergence of domination and resistance

The building of the Assyrian Empire

A series of political, economic, and military developments that occurred around the beginning of the 9th century BC planted the seeds for the major military conflicts of Israel and Judah throughout the next three centuries. Just before 900, Assyria lingered in a decline that had characterized the preceding century. The central administration in the heartland had suffered from a series of weak rulers and was in disarray, and Aramean groups in Syria had driven Assyrian influence back across the Euphrates to the east. The Assyrians were, as one king's annals recorded, a "toil-worn people." The first hint of recovery began in the years 934–884, with a sequence of three rulers named Ashur-dan II, Adad-nirari II, and Tukulti-ninurta II. Their reigns were relatively short but effective. They reestablished security around the Assyrian heartland, effected economic growth, and expanded the borders northwest toward the Euphrates and south toward Babylon.

However, the birth of the so-called "Neo-Assyrian Empire" truly began with a king named Ashurnasirpal II in 883. He undertook 14 major campaigns during his 24-year reign. His goals included achieving control of the crossings of the Euphrates and other major trade routes, acquiring tribute, material goods, and captives, as well as establishing trade colonies in the west. While his campaigns focused on the territory of northern Syria

King Ashurnasirpal II of Assyria (883–859 BC) pictured in a statue of 3ft 6in (1m). The 14 major campaigns during his reign gave birth to the "Neo-Assyrian Empire" and extended its influence westward to the Mediterranean Sea. (akg-images/Erich Lessing)

A stone relief from the palace of Ashurnasirpal showing the king's guards. (Werner Forman Archive)

around the Euphrates, they secured a perimeter around the Assyrian heartland in every direction: the Zagros mountains to the east, the area of Lake Van to the north, the middle Euphrates to the south, and the Kingdom of Bit-Adini to the west. Probably as a result of these successes, the heartland flourished and Ashurnasirpal became known for significant, even extravagant, building activities. For example, he built a new capital at Calah (Nimrud) and dedicated it with a celebration that his annals say included over 47,000 guests and 5,000 dignitaries from various regions:

When I inaugurated the palace at Calah I treated for ten days with food and drink 47,074 persons, men and women, who were bid to come from across my entire country, (also) 5,000 important persons, delegates … (also) 16,000 inhabitants of Calah from all ways of life, 1,500 officials of all my palaces.[20]

It was this aggressive Assyrian expansion beyond the Euphrates that set the stage for the conflicts with kingdoms in Syria-Palestine. Ashurnasirpal's inscriptions state that the Assyrians pushed into

Phoenician territory along the coast of the Mediterranean Sea for the first time in 875, after traversing northern Syria. The king received tribute from all major rulers of northern Syria and Phoenicia, as far south as Tyre. Although some of these payments may have represented the voluntary establishment of trade relations and not subjugation, Ashurnasirpal was the first king to bring a powerful Assyrian presence into the western part of the Fertile Crescent.

Ashurnasirpal did not, however, incorporate these kingdoms into the Assyrian Empire in a systematic way. That task fell to his son and successor, Shalmaneser III (859–824). In a series of annual campaigns over his first six years, the new king immediately embarked on an effort not only to secure Assyria's dominance in northern Syria, but also to bring the kingdoms in southern Syria-Palestine under Assyrian influence. Several royal inscriptions note that in his first year, for example, Shalmaneser followed the path of his predecessor and marched to the Mediterranean Sea, where he erected an image of himself. On this campaign, he moved into the area of Bit-Adini and the cities of Til-Barsip and Carchemish, where he encountered a northern Syrian coalition of four kingdoms (Sama'al, Patin, Bit-Adini, and Carchemish). Although the size of the armies involved is not known, the Assyrians captured various parts of coalition territory.

Although subdued, the northern Syrian coalition was not destroyed, and these kingdoms continued to try to halt Shalmaneser's movements in the west at various strategic points around the Habur and Euphrates rivers. Thus, in his second year, Shalmaneser returned west to subjugate and collect tribute from areas not conquered in his first year. He also recaptured Carchemish and engaged Ahuni of Bit-Adini. By the end of the second year, the Assyrians had confined Ahuni to his capital at Til-Barsip and laid siege to the city, but had not captured it. Shalmaneser's third year, however, saw the final capture of Til-Barsip and thus the ultimate establishment of Assyrian dominance in northern Syria. He turned Til-Barsip into an Assyrian royal city named "Kar-Shalmaneser," built palaces within it, and repopulated it with Assyrians. Although the ruler Ahuni evaded capture for one more year, Shalmaneser received tribute from the kings throughout the seacoast, solidified Assyrian domination of northern Syria, and returned east to attack Urartu.

A power in Israel

During the very years of Assyria's developing dominance in Phoenicia and northern Syria, Israel and other southern Syro-Palestinian kingdoms such as Damascus and Hamath experienced newfound political and economic growth, which set them on a collision course with Assyria. For Israel, this growth began in the first half of the 9th century with the "Omride Dynasty." Omri (879–869), a ranking officer in the Israelite army, ascended to the throne shortly after the beginning of Ashurnasirpal's reign in Assyria. Omri and his son, Ahab (869–853), oversaw the Kingdom of Israel's greatest period of domestic prosperity and political prominence. Together they made significant strides in the areas of military strength, territorial expansion, and political alliances.

Biblical texts about Omri and Ahab emphasize their unfaithfulness to Israel's God, with only incidental references to building projects and no descriptions of their military and political undertakings that are detailed in Assyrian and Moabite inscriptions.[21] Their religious unfaithfulness particularly involved promoting worship of the god Baal, a Phoenician deity associated with fertility of crops and animals. This sponsorship may have resulted from close political ties to Phoenicia, since Ahab took a Phoenician princess as queen. But even within this religious focus, the biblical narratives provide some details about Omri's rise. Around the time of Ashurnasirpal's accession, Israel's army was attacking the Philistine city of Gibbethon approximately 30 miles (48km) southwest of Samaria, while Elah, the King of Israel, remained in his capital at Tirzah. Zimri, the commander of half of Israel's chariotry, assassinated Elah in the capital and reigned in his place. After only seven days, however, the army proclaimed Omri, the commander of the Israelite infantry, king. He besieged Zimri in Tirzah, and Zimri burned the palace down upon himself in suicide. Upon that event, a civil war broke out in Israel between Omri and a rival claimant to the throne, named Tibni. No details about the war are known, but it may have involved opposing factions of Israel's military, namely, the general army (supporting Omri) and the chariot corps (supporting Tibni). Resolution came at the end of about four years, and Omri secured the Israelite throne by 879.

During the following two and a half decades, when Ashurnasirpal and Shalmaneser were solidifying Assyrian dominance over northern Syria, Omri and Ahab achieved a measure of domestic prosperity and political power for Israel. Archeology attests significant building activities by these rulers, most importantly Omri's founding of Samaria as the new capital of Israel,[22] a site located closer to the main north–south route through Syria-Palestine to Egypt. Extensive Omride construction phases also appear at key cities

The foundation of a portion of the 9th-century BC city wall at the Israelite capital of Samaria. The construction of this city as the capital of Israel was the work of King Omri. (Todd Bolen/BiblePlaces.com)

like Megiddo, Hazor, and Jezreel; and Omri and Ahab were perhaps responsible for monumental architecture at other sites previously thought to be from the 10th century.

Israel's political prominence under Omri and Ahab involved cooperation with and dominance over neighboring kingdoms. The HB/OT says Israel established an alliance with Phoenicia, symbolized by the marriage of Ahab and Jezebel, the daughter of the king of Sidon: "he [Ahab] took as his wife Jezebel daughter of King Ethbaal of the Sidonians..."[23] The "Mesha Inscription," a text from King Mesha of Moab that comes from after the death of Ahab (c.853), notes that Omri had conquered Moabite territory north of the Arnon River because of the displeasure of Moab's god Kemosh, and celebrates Mesha's later liberation of that area:

Omri was the king of Israel, and he oppressed Moab for many days, for Kemosh was angry with his land. And his son succeeded him, and he said – he too – "I will oppress Moab!" In my days did he say [so], but I looked down on him and on his house, and Israel has gone to ruin, yes, it has gone to ruin forever![24]

Biblical texts likewise describe annual tribute paid to Israel by Mesha[25] and suggest that a "deputy" of Israel or Judah governed Edom.[26] Omri or Ahab may also have campaigned successfully against Aram-Damascus, perhaps before 860, although this is not certain. The background for this possible campaign was the earlier reign of Baasha of Israel (903–882), when the Aramean king Ben-Hadad I seized territories in northern Israel around Dan: "he [Ben-Hadad I] conquered Ijon, Dan, Abel-beth-maacah, and all Chinneroth, with all the land of Naphtali."[27] The HB/OT does not indicate when Israel regained these holdings, and it may have been under Omri or Ahab. The opening lines of an Aramaic inscription from Tel Dan, which comes from

Expansion campaigns of Shalmaneser III 858–853 BC

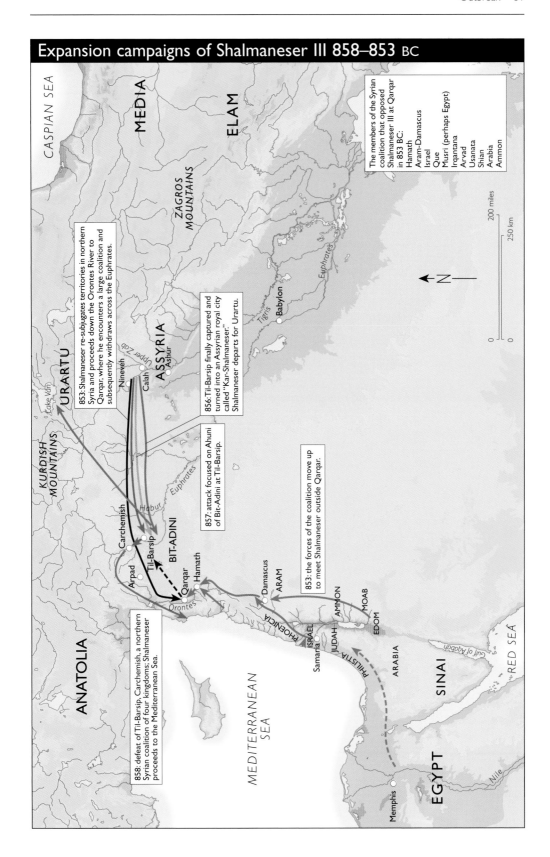

The members of the Syrian coalition that opposed Shalmaneser III at Qarqar in 853 BC:
Hamath
Aram–Damascus
Israel
Que
Musri (perhaps Egypt)
Irqantana
Arvad
Usanata
Shian
Arabia
Ammon

853: Shalmaneser re-subjugates territories in northern Syria and proceeds down the Orontes River to Qarqar, where he encounters a large coalition and subsequently withdraws across the Euphrates.

856: Til-Barsip finally captured and turned into an Assyrian royal city called "Kar-Shalmaneser." Shalmaneser departs for Urartu.

857: attack focused on Ahuni of Bit-Adini at Til-Barsip.

853: the forces of the coalition move up to meet Shalmaneser outside Qarqar.

858: defeat of Til-Barsip, Carchemish, a northern Syrian coalition of four kingdoms; Shalmaneser proceeds to the Mediterranean Sea.

200 miles
250 km

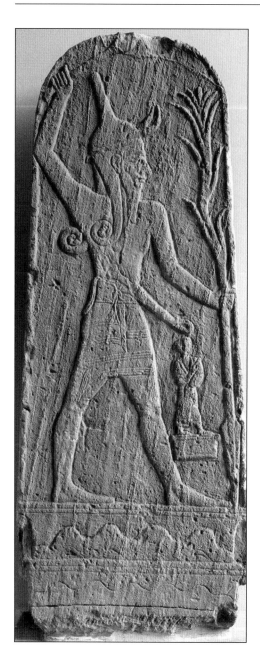

A depiction of the Canaanite god "Baal" found at the city of Ugarit. Sponsorship of Baal worship, rather than military and political achievements, is the focus of the biblical accounts of the Israelite kings Omri and Ahab in the 9th century BC. (R Sheridan, Ancient Art and Architecture Collection Ltd)

Links with Judah

While the ascendancy under Omri and Ahab centered on Israel, Judah experienced similar developments, and the history of the two kingdoms corresponded closely during this period. Judah, as a smaller, more remote, and less-developed kingdom, benefited from Israel's economic prosperity and political security. The HB/OT links the two kingdoms by an alliance established by the marriage of Athaliah, daughter of either Omri or Ahab,[29] to Jehoram, son of the Judean king, Jehoshaphat (877–853). Furthermore, biblical and non-biblical inscriptions suggest that the Omrides may have reduced Judah to near-vassal status. The HB/OT remembers Jehoshaphat as a king who placed the Judean military at the disposal of Ahab[30] and who "made peace with" or "surrendered to" Israel.[31] Likewise, Assyrian inscriptions throughout this period refer to several Israelite rulers but never mention a Judean king until nearly the end of the 8th century.

Within the first half of the 9th century, Israel under Omri and Ahab became a major player in the political scene of southern Syria-Palestine, with significant influence, if not control, over several neighboring territories. Such burgeoning economic and political strength among kingdoms like Damascus, Hamath, and Israel destined them to collide with the increasing Assyrian dominance in the north.

the later Aramean king, Hazael (c.843–805), mentions an Israelite invasion of Aram during the time of his predecessor, and this may be a reference to an Israelite campaign in the time of Omri or Ahab:

...my father went u[p against him when] he fought at x[ ]. Then my father lay down and went to his [fathers]. There came up the king of I[s]rael beforetime in the land of my father...[28]

Creating crisis

The ultimate catalyst for the outbreak of conflict in Syria-Palestine came in 856, when Shalmaneser III finally captured Til-Barsip in Bit-Adini and achieved a secure political and economic dominance over the area.

The Mesha Inscription of King Mesha of Moab in the 9th century BC that describes Omri of Israel's subjugation of Moabite territory and Mesha's subsequent liberation of that territory after the death of Omri's son, Ahab. (akg-images/Erich Lessing)

Assyria's final subjugation of northern Syria undoubtedly signaled an immediate threat to the southern kingdoms. In response, about a dozen of these kingdoms forged an alliance, which was headed by the three powers of Aram-Damascus, Hamath, and Israel. Together they sought to resist Assyrian domination of trade routes and commercial resources.

Shalmaneser's immediate departure to Urartu after subduing northern Syria in 856 provided the space needed to organize the coalition. His inscriptions attest, however, that in 853 he set his sights on Syria-Palestine. The Assyrian army at first moved once more against northern territories like Carchemish and Aleppo, but then began a new thrust to the south by approaching the town of Qarqar, the gateway to Hamath, Damascus, and southern Syria-Palestine. At Qarqar, Shalmaneser encountered the coalition of southern kingdoms, including the forces of Ahab of Israel. The confrontation was the first of seven campaigns that Shalmaneser would make into Syria-Palestine, and it set in motion a series of conflicts that would engulf the Ancient Near East over the next two centuries.

In the maelstrom of empires

Israel and Assyria (853 BC)

By the early spring of 853, the Kingdom
of Israel under Ahab stood beside
Aram-Damascus and Hamath as one
of the three major powers in central
and southern Syria. Hamath, under King
Irhuleni, dominated the territory north
of Tyre around the Orontes River, while
Aram-Damascus, under King Hadadezer
(or Adad-idri), dominated the area south of
Hamath and east of the Jordan River. Israel
held much of the inland territory south of
Tyre and Sidon and west of the Jordan River.
The northern kingdom had also possibly
relegated the southern Kingdom of Judah
to virtual vassal status.

Throughout most of the preceding
two decades, these three regional powers
had cooperated with one another at least
indirectly. Although some biblical texts
locate hostilities between Israel and
Aram-Damascus during the reign of Ahab,[32]
the historical details of these texts fit better
with the next phase of Israelite history,
and the texts have probably misidentified
the Israelite king originally involved. In any
case, the three kingdoms were able to control
the flow of commerce without interference
from outside powers, including Assyria,
which remained preoccupied with continued
resistance in northern Syria. Quite naturally
then, when the Assyrian king Shalmaneser III
decisively eliminated the north Syrian power
of Til-Barsip in 856, the southern powers of
Hamath, Aram-Damascus, and Israel realized
the imminent threat to their well-being
and formed a coalition to resist Assyrian
advancement into southern Syria.

In the summer months of 853, after
conquering the area between the Tigris and
Euphrates and reasserting dominance over
northern Syrian cities like Carchemish and
Aleppo, Shalmaneser turned the Assyrian
army south into the territory controlled by
Irhuleni of Hamath. Shalmaneser's Monolith
Inscription, the primary source for this
campaign, describes the systematic
destruction of Irhuleni's royal cities
as the Assyrian army moved down the
Orontes River toward the city of Qarqar:

I approached the cities of Irhuleni, the
Hamathite. I captured Adennu, Pargâ, (and)
Arganâ, his royal cities. I carried off captives,
his valuables, (and) his palace possessions. I set
fire to his palaces. I departed from the city of
Arganâ. I approached the city of Qarqar.[33]

The Assyrians meet the coalition at Qarqar

The town of Qarqar, located on the east bank
of the Orontes, was a mere 30 to 40 miles
(50–60km) northwest of Hamath, and
represented the gateway to southern Syria.
With no recorded substantial resistance,
the Assyrians conquered and burned
Qarqar. When he set out to continue
his march south, however, Shalmaneser
confronted an extremely large coalition
fully drawn up to aid Irhuleni and stop
Assyria's entrance into southern Syria.

Hamath, Aram-Damascus, and Israel
constituted the primary partners, but the
coalition against Shalmaneser consisted
of around a dozen kingdoms from central
Syria, Syria-Palestine, northern Phoenicia,
the Transjordan, Arabia, and perhaps Egypt,
although the presence of that name in
inscriptions remains uncertain. Many of
these kingdoms had ties with Hamath and
shared its concern to protect trade routes
into central and southern Syria. The Assyrian
records also detail the coalition kingdoms'
numbers of chariotry, infantry, and cavalry.

A captured Judean chariot being led away by Assyrian soldiers after the battle of Lachish in 701 BC. This is the only known representation of a Judean chariot (which looks identical to the Assyrian chariot), although biblical and extra-biblical texts consistently mention Israelite and Judean chariot forces. (British Museum, London)

If these records are accurate, the coalition force was massive and probably significantly outnumbered the Assyrian army. According to the Assyrians, Hamath, Aram-Damascus, and Israel alone fielded 40,000 soldiers, 1,900 cavalry, and 3,900 chariots, with the other members contributing more than 22,000 additional soldiers plus chariots. By comparison, just a decade later (c.843), records indicate that the Assyrian army possessed only about 2,000 chariots and 5,500 cavalry. Assyrian inscriptions often exaggerated and rounded numbers for propagandistic purposes, however, and some of the forces seem out of keeping with what is known of the populations for the areas in the mid-9th century. Such exaggerations probably served the purpose of making Assyria's power seem even greater in victory, and providing ready explanations when victory was not clear.

Of particular interest is the army attributed to Ahab of Israel: 10,000 soldiers, 700 cavalry, and 2,000 chariots – the largest chariot force in the coalition and one that was equal to that of Assyria at the height of its power in the following decade. The population estimates of the city of Samaria for this period suggest that Israel would have fielded a much smaller army, and even if one identifies stables in the archeological record at Israelite cities like Megiddo, there remains a lack of evidence for adequate horse facilities to support so large a chariot force. Hence, some historians have suggested that the number of Israel's forces was mistakenly recorded or deliberately multiplied by perhaps as many as ten.

A better explanation can be derived from the fact that Assyrian records of this battle make no mention of Israel's immediate neighbors of Judah, Moab, and Edom, kingdoms described elsewhere as being under the influence, and perhaps even under the control, of Israel during this period. For example, biblical texts, while not mentioning the battle of Qarqar, portray Judah during this time as bound by a treaty relationship to Israel through the marriage of a northern princess to a southern prince.[34] The Phoenician cities of Tyre and Sidon, which like Judah also go unmentioned in Assyrian records of the battle, also had a treaty relationship with Israel signified by the marriage of Ahab to Jezebel, daughter of the King of Sidon. Thus, another possible explanation for the size of Israel's forces at Qarqar is that kingdoms like Judah, Moab, Edom, and perhaps Phoenicia contributed contingents that were counted under the banner of Israel.

Whatever the exact numbers, the Syro-Palestinian coalition presented a formidable force. The Assyrians had a tactical advantage, however, since the battlefield was near the territory of Bit-Agusi and other northern cities that had capitulated to Assyrian control. Nonetheless, the size of the coalition armies, combined with the likely depletion of Assyrian forces from earlier battles on the campaign, tipped the scales in favor of the alliance. Assyrian records indicate a bloody battle. They place the total of slain coalition troops at varying numbers between 14,000 and 29,000, and Shalmaneser describes piling up enough corpses to stop up the Orontes River and form a bridge across it:

I decisively defeated them from the city of Qarqar to the city of Gilzau. I felled with the sword 14,000 troops, their fighting men... I spread out their corpses (and) I filled the plain. [I felled] with the sword their extensive troops. I made their blood flow... The field was too small for laying flat their bodies ... the broad countryside had been consumed in burying them. I blocked the Orontes River with their corpses as

The Monolith Inscription of King Shalmaneser III of Assyria containing an inscription written over the relief of the king. This inscription is the main source for the battle of Qarqar in 853, which involved King Ahab of Israel but is not mentioned in the Bible. (British Museum, London)

with a causeway. In the midst of this battle I took away from them chariots, cavalry, (and) teams of horses.[35]

There is reason to believe, however, that Qarqar was at least a stalemate if not a victory by Israel and its coalition partners. Shalmaneser did not press south of Qarqar in 853 and did not even campaign west of the Euphrates for the next three years. When the Assyrians finally did return to the west in 849, their annals record that they had to re-take north Syrian territories like Bit-Agusi and Carchemish, and battle the same Syro-Palestinian coalition on three more occasions.

Seen in a broad perspective, the coalition's confrontation at Qarqar with the Assyrians was the most significant battle that took place in the Levant in the 9th century, and represented the pinnacle of Israel's power during that period. Ahab's ability to contribute one of the most significant military contingents to this battle was the fruit of several decades of prosperity. This action solidified Israel's status as a regional power, and set it on a course of cooperation with its neighbors against Assyria that would last until regional politics shifted dramatically at the end of the next decade.

Israel and Aram-Damascus (843–805)

The next major conflicts in Israelite and Judean history involved a series of confrontations with Aram-Damascus that spanned nearly the entire second half of the 9th century.

Ahab of Israel apparently died sometime shortly after the battle of Qarqar. Although the sequence of kings is confusing for the following years, Israel's and Judah's fortunes clearly changed for the worse. Shalmaneser returned to the west on three more occasions in 849, 848, and 845 and faced the same coalition of southern kingdoms each time. Assyrian records continue to name Irhuleni and Hadadezer as the coalition leaders, but do not refer to Ahab's successors Ahaziah or Jehoram. Since it is likely that Israel continued to participate in the coalition, the lack of reference may reflect a deterioration in its power.

Both biblical and extra-biblical texts show that many of the kingdoms that had been under Ahab's control in 853 rebelled after his death: "After the death of Ahab, Moab rebelled against Israel… In his [Jehoram's] days Edom revolted against the rule of Judah, and set up a king of their own."[36] For example, an inscription of King Mesha of Moab claims that he successfully drove the Israelites out of Moabite territory east of the Jordan River and north of the Wadi Arnon.

Mesha may have joined with the Ammonites to invade Judah by crossing the Dead Sea, taking the coastal city of Ein Gedi, and marching into the wilderness southeast of Jerusalem. The HB/OT suggests that Jehoram of Israel and Jehoshaphat of Judah led a combined Israelite and Judean retaliatory strike into Moab by marching around the south end of the Dead Sea, through Edom, and laying siege to Kir-hareseth near Dibon, the capital of Moab.[37] The route itself was prohibitive, marked by dangerous desert heat and drought, and the biblical narrative indicates that the army was saved from destruction by a flash flood in a canyon:

So the King of Israel, the King of Judah, and the King of Edom set out; and when they had made a roundabout march of seven days, there was no water for the army or for the animals that were with them… And he [Elisha] said, 'Thus says the LORD, I will make this wadi full of pools'… The next day, about the time of the morning offering, suddenly water began to flow from the direction of Edom, until the country was filled with water.[38]

Although the army succeeded in destroying some cities in southern Moab, they were unable to conquer Kir-hareseth or press on to Dibon, the capital. The biblical account attributes the Israelite defeat to King Mesha's sacrifice of his son on the city wall.

Even with a weakened Israel, in the 840s the coalition as a whole was successful in turning back the Assyrian army at the Orontes River on all three occasions when they advanced to that point. The balance of power in the west changed radically, however, when a new king named Hazael came to the throne in Damascus around 843. Assyrian texts designate him a usurper, and biblical texts imply that he murdered his predecessor. Hazael may have interpreted the steady decline in Israel's power and Shalmaneser's inability to push below the Orontes as signs that Aram-Damascus could gain power over all of southern Syria-Palestine. Perhaps for this reason, Hazael immediately reversed the existing

A band relief showing the Assyrian army of Shalmaneser III on campaign in Phoenicia (c.850). The top band depicts tribute being brought to the Assyrians by inhabitants of the coastal city of Tyre. The bottom band shows the army on campaign against Hazazu. (© 2003, Topham PicturePoint/Topfoto.co.uk)

political alignments and initiated hostilities against Israel in the Transjordan territory around Ramoth-gilead, a move that probably brought about the collapse of what remained of the old coalition. Although no descriptions of the battle have survived, 2 Kings 8 records that Jehoram, the King of Israel, was wounded in this battle and retreated to Jezreel leaving Jehu, one of the commanders of the army, in charge of the forces at Ramoth-gilead.

While Israelite forces were defending Ramoth-gilead against Aram-Damascus in 841, Shalmaneser led the Assyrian army back to the west for a fifth time. This time, however, he did not meet the old coalition but only Hazael of Damascus. With no coalition to check its advance at the Orontes, the Assyrian army probably marched through the Beqa' valley to Damascus. Hazael withdrew from Ramoth-gilead and made his stand at a peak near Mount Lebanon. Assyrian texts claim the defeat of 16,000 Aramean soldiers,

1,121 chariots, and 470 cavalry. The Assyrians pushed Hazael back to the capital city of Damascus but chose not to place the city under siege, a choice that would have long-lasting consequences for the west. Shalmaneser's army devastated the surrounding lands, cities, and villages and proceeded to a mountain on the Mediterranean coast in the vicinity of Tyre.

The events of the clash between Hazael and Shalmaneser overlapped one of the most significant developments in Israelite history. With the wounded Jehoram cloistered in Jezreel, the Israelite army at Ramoth-gilead proclaimed Jehu king, an accession that the HB/OT presents as a religious revolution motivated by the desire to eliminate the House of Ahab that had allowed worship of the Phoenician god Baal.[39] According to the biblical story, Jehu promptly attacked Jehoram at Jezreel, as well as the Judean king Ahaziah who had joined him there, killing Jehoram in the open field and wounding the fleeing Ahaziah who later died at Megiddo. Jehu then sent letters to the capital city Samaria, and secured by threat the capitulation of the city's officials and garrison. The Aramaic inscription from Tel Dan appears to give credit for the killings of these kings to Hazael rather than Jehu, leaving open the question of who the driving force was behind these actions.

In any case, upon his coup, Jehu faced the choice of renewing the alliance with Aram-Damascus that had turned back the Assyrians just four years earlier, or following the lead of many other regional kingdoms and submitting to Shalmaneser. Jehu opted to present himself before Shalmaneser and establish Israel as an Assyrian vassal. This submission is memorialized in relief and writing on the Assyrian Black Obelisk, the only surviving visual representation of an Israelite or Judean king:

I received the tribute of Jehu ... (the man) of Bit-Humrî : silver, gold, a golden bowl, a golden goblet, golden cups, golden buckets, tin, a staff of the king's hand, (and) javelins(?)[40]

This pro-Assyrian alignment would be Israel's dominant posture for nearly a century. As is typical for this period,

A panel of the Black Obelisk of King Shalmaneser III of Assyria that depicts the Israelite king, Jehu, submitting and paying tribute (c.841 BC). Jehu kneels, with his representatives behind him bearing gifts, and Shalmaneser stands to the left of the kneeling king. (akg-images/Erich Lessing)

biblical texts picture Judah as a weaker partner that followed the northern kingdom's foreign policy.

Thus, Hazael was defeated by Assyria in 841 but, unfortunately for Israel, not destroyed. Shalmaneser returned to the west to check Hazael once more in 838–837. He captured some Aramean cities but still did not remove Hazael or do extensive damage to his kingdom. Following this campaign, however, Assyria entered a period of decline and was unable to return to the west for the next 30 years. The Egyptians during this period were likewise entangled in internal conflicts and played no significant role in Syria-Palestine.

In this vacuum between 837 and 810, Hazael established a mini-empire that encompassed the central Palestinian hill country, Transjordan, Syria, and Philistia. He seems to have relegated Israel and Judah to vassal-like status. Virtually no details are known for any one battle, but the overall course of events is clear. Archeological evidence of destruction is visible at key Israelite cities like Jezreel, and biblical texts explicitly describe the loss of Transjordanian territory and the continual subjugation of Israel and Judah by Damascus:[41] "The anger of the LORD was kindled against Israel, so

that he gave them repeatedly into the hand of King Hazael of Aram, then into the hand of Ben-Hadad son of Hazael."[42] Aramaic inscriptions may even indicate that Hazael campaigned into Assyrian territory north of the Euphrates, and that his son and successor, Ben-Hadad II, tried to extend Aramean dominance over Hamath in northern Syria.

Israel and Judah suffered militarily and economically during this time. Late in this period (c.820), for example, 2 Kings 13: 7 credits Jehoahaz, Jehu's successor, with an army of fewer than 50 horsemen, 10 chariots, and 10,000 soldiers. The turning point came, however, in 810, when Adad-nirari III took the throne in Assyria and initiated a resurgence in the Empire's strength. After securing matters in Assyria, Adad-nirari came west in 805 and established his base of operations at Arpad in northern Syria for a multi-directional, three-year campaign. This resurgence allowed Israel to throw off the yoke of Aram-Damascus, a liberation that probably began under Jehoahaz. Biblical accounts like 2 Kings 13 and 1 Kings 20 and 22 suggest the possible scenario that, around 805, Ben-Hadad marched south to the Jordan Valley and sent demands to Samaria, but the Israelites turned back the Aramean forces. The next spring, the Arameans returned south but were met by an Israelite army at Aphek near the Jezreel Valley. The Israelites won a sound victory, the HB/OT says, killing 28,000 enemy soldiers and capturing Ben-Hadad. He was later released upon agreeing to relinquish captured Israelite territory. Some time later, biblical texts say that Jehoahaz led a joint Israelite and Judean force to Ramoth-gilead in order to reclaim territory that Ben-Hadad had promised to relinquish. The Israelite king was mortally wounded in the battle, and Joash succeeded him. Although the time span is unclear, Joash seems to have defeated Ben-Hadad on three subsequent occasions and ended Aramean oppression of Israel for the time being. The Assyrians then subjugated Damascus sometime between 805 and 802 but did not destroy the city or remove Ben-Hadad from the throne, perhaps thinking that this

A relief with accompanying inscription of King Adad-nirari III of Assyria, who led the Assyrian resurgence in the west after 810 BC. He subdued Ben-Hadad II of Aram-Damascus and allowed Israel to break free of Aramean control. (akg-images/Erich Lessing)

would evoke his loyalty. Upon this show of force, several local kings paid tribute and reaffirmed their loyalty to Assyria. Among these kings was Joash of Israel.

Throughout these events, Judah probably continued to play the role of lesser partner to Israel. Upon liberation from Aram-Damascus, a new Judean king named Amaziah inherited the throne from his father Jehoash (c.802). According to the biblical story, after capturing some Edomite territory east of Beersheba, Amaziah challenged Joash of Israel.[43] Although Judah was the instigator, the battle took place in

Judean territory near Beth-shemesh, west of Jerusalem. Joash captured Jerusalem, broke down a section of the city's wall, looted the temple and treasuries, and took Amaziah prisoner to Samaria. While Joash later returned the Judean king to his throne, this conflict between the sister kingdoms foreshadowed things to come.

Israel, Aram-Damascus, and Judah: the Syro-Ephraimitic War (734–731 BC)

With a resurgent Assyria after 805, loyal Assyrian vassals like Israel experienced a time of recovery, which took place during the first half of the reign of Jeroboam II of Israel (788–748). The biblical account indicates that Jeroboam recovered the commercial port of Elath from the Arameans, which opened the Red Sea trading route, and 8th-century archeological remains at Israelite cities show an increased presence of luxury items that may date to Jeroboam's time. Israel also probably expanded its borders northward to the Beqa' valley and southward to the Dead Sea, expansions which are likely to have been made at the expense of Damascus and Hamath:

He restored the border of Israel from Lebo-hamath as far as the Sea of the Arabah [Dead Sea], according to the word of the LORD, the God of Israel, which he spoke by his servant Jonah son of Amittai, the prophet...[44]

The Judean kings Uzziah and Jotham reigned under the shadow of Jeroboam and probably shared in the prosperity. The HB/OT claims that Uzziah expanded Judah's army to 307,500 soldiers and scored victories over the Philistines, Arabs, and others.

Much of Israel's success at this time was probably due to a change in Assyrian administrative methods. Adad-nirari placed power in the west into the hands of field marshals who maintained a direct Assyrian military presence in the region. But Assyria fell into decline during the reigns of

Adad-nirari's successors (c.780–750). Powerful field marshals disappeared from the scene by about 750, removing the strong Assyrian presence and creating a vacuum of power. Around the year 750, a new ruler named Rezin (or Radyan), who came from a provincial town outside the capital, usurped the throne in Damascus and proved that Assyria had made a mistake by not destroying Aram-Damascus in preceding years. Rezin's actions suggest that he had visions of reestablishing Hazael's mini-empire of a century earlier and liberating the west from Assyrian dominance. It seems possible that he seized control of Israelite territory in the Transjordan and Galilee as early as the 750s.[45] He also appears to have assisted Edom in recapturing the port of Elath, and to have opened the door for the Philistines to encroach on Judean territory in the Shephelah and Negeb.

These events had severe consequences for Israel and Judah. The available sources record a series of subsequent actions that suggest the population was divided into opposing factions, with a large segment in both kingdoms favoring the Damascus-led movement to throw off the Assyrian yoke. In Israel, for example, after the death of Jeroboam in 748, four kings reigned in quick succession between the years 748 and 734, and three of them were killed after short reigns. The central government in Samaria continually lost territory to surrounding kingdoms that were rallying to Rezin's cause.[46] Most significantly, Rezin seems to have fostered the emergence of a pro-Damascus rival claimant to the throne in Israel named Pekah, a Gileadite from the region just south of Aram-Damascus. The HB/OT remembers Pekah as being active alongside Rezin in the northern Transjordan as early as the 750s while Jeroboam was still king in Samaria.[47] Perhaps Pekah became the puppet ruler of the Transjordan and Galilee when Rezin seized those territories after 750.

The event that precipitated the outbreak of direct hostilities among Israel, Aram-Damascus, and Judah, however, came in 745. After years of decline, a general named Pul usurped the throne in Assyria and took the name Tiglath-pileser III. He immediately undertook military campaigns designed to reestablish Assyrian dominance over the north and west. He also instituted a new policy of relocating conquered peoples, annexing conquered kingdoms as imperial provinces, and establishing permanent military bases in conquered areas.

Tiglath-pileser came west in 743, and established the region around Arpad as a base for a four-year campaign throughout northern Syria. During this campaign, Assyrian texts note that Tiglath-pileser received tribute from Syro-Palestinian kings including Tubail of Tyre, Menahem of Israel, and even Rezin of Damascus. These payments were probably offered only as nominal tribute designed to avoid direct confrontation, since Tiglath-pileser was not yet moving into southern Syria. Assyria's only involvement in the south came when Tiglath-pileser sent troops to help Menahem of Israel secure the throne of Samaria, especially in light of the rival claimant Pekah: "King Pul [Tiglath-pileser III] of Assyria came against the land; Menahem gave Pul a thousand talents of silver, so that he might help him confirm his hold on the royal power."[48]

By 737, however, Tiglath-pileser had annexed 19 districts of Hamath and won a conclusive victory over northern Syria. Rezin and his supporters no doubt saw these developments as a sign that an Assyrian move into southern Syria was now inevitable. Thus, when Tiglath-pileser withdrew northward to fight Urartu in 735, Rezin solidified an anti-Assyrian coalition including Tyre, Gaza, Ashkelon, Arabia, and others. As part of this development, the rival claimant Pekah finally made his move on the Israelite throne. He apparently assassinated the sitting king, took control of Samaria, and joined the coalition in 734.[49] Although 2 Kings 15: 27 says he went on to reign 20 years, the chronology of biblical and Assyrian texts suggests this number includes his years as a rival claimant. More importantly, for the first time in over a century, the official foreign policy of the northern kingdom became anti-Assyrian. In the same year, Egyptian inscriptions indicate that the Ethiopian king Piye sailed northward on the Nile, conquered Memphis, and extended his dominance into the Egyptian Delta. This campaign, particularly designed to curb the expansion of Tefnakht of Sais, did not achieve hegemony over the Delta but probably

A relief from the Assyrian royal palace at Calah that shows the Assyrian king Tiglath-pileser III (left) holding a bow and standing over a kneeling vassal (c.745–727). (© 2004, Detroit Institute of Arts/Founders Society Purchase, Ralph Harman Booth Bequest Fund (50.32))

Campaigns of Tiglath-pileser III 743–738 BC and 734–731 BC

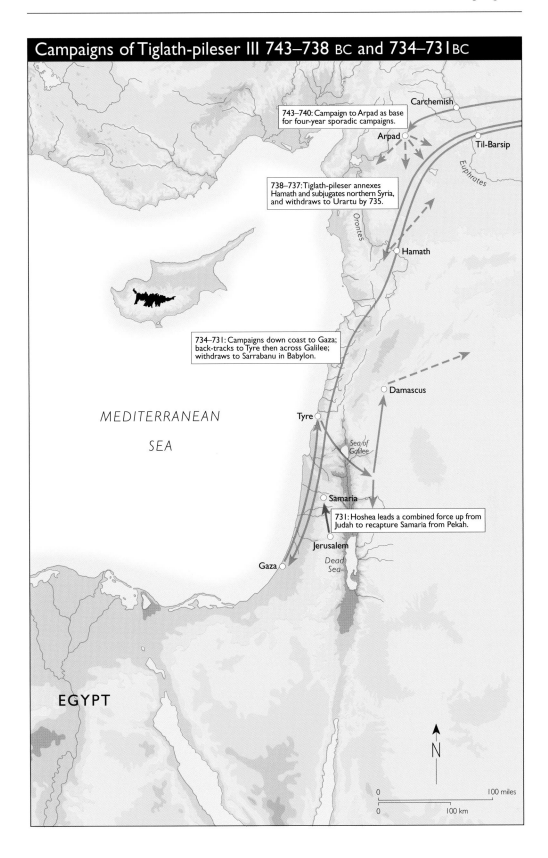

743–740: Campaign to Arpad as base for four-year sporadic campaigns.

738–737: Tiglath-pileser annexes Hamath and subjugates northern Syria, and withdraws to Urartu by 735.

734–731: Campaigns down coast to Gaza; back-tracks to Tyre then across Galilee; withdraws to Sarrabanu in Babylon.

731: Hoshea leads a combined force up from Judah to recapture Samaria from Pekah.

Carchemish

Arpad

Til-Barsip

Euphrates

Orontes

Hamath

Damascus

MEDITERRANEAN

SEA

Tyre

Sea of Galilee

Samaria

Jerusalem

Gaza

Dead Sea

EGYPT

N

0   100 miles

0   100 km

secured the trade routes into Philistia and Lebanon. To the eyes of the budding Syro-Palestinian coalition it must have been a sign that Assyrian power was ready to slip.

For the first time since before the reign of Omri, however, the southern kingdom of Judah apparently did not follow the northern kingdom's lead. After Pekah's coup in Samaria, the Assyrian records that show the withholding of tribute by coalition members contain the first reference to a tribute payment by any king of Judah. This payment probably meant that King Ahaz of Judah, who had inherited the throne from his father Jotham, refused to join the coalition and prevented Rezin from establishing a united front against the Assyrians.

In response, probably before Tiglath-pileser was out of the region in early 734, Rezin and Pekah besieged Jerusalem, initiating the so-called "Syro-Ephraimitic War." Several biblical texts describe the details of this siege, even including purported conversations between Ahaz and the prophet Isaiah:

In the days of Ahaz son of Jotham son of Uzziah, king of Judah, King Rezin of Aram and King Pekah son of Remaliah of Israel went up to attack Jerusalem, but could not mount an attack against it....[T]herefore thus says the Lord GOD: It shall not stand, and it shall not come to pass.[50]

The express aim of Syria and Ephraim's (i.e. Israel's) actions was to replace Ahaz with a compliant ruler and return Judah to its vassal-like role in relation to Israel. There may have been an unsuccessful assassination attempt on Ahaz by an Ephraimite operative just prior to the siege in 734.[51] Isaiah 10: 27d–32 perhaps details the route of the Aramean and Israelite force: they traveled south by an interior road east of Samaria that passed through Michmash and Gibeon and ended at Nob, about a mile (roughly 2km) east of Jerusalem. This was the more geographically difficult but less fortified path from Samaria to Jerusalem.

By this time, however, the anti-Assyrian actions in Syria-Palestine had attracted Tiglath-pileser's attention. In late 734 or early 733, the Assyrians swept down the length of the Mediterranean coast to Gaza, probably to seal off the Egyptian border and prevent any possible involvement by Piye of Ethiopia. Thus began a three-year campaign to deal with Rezin's coalition (734–731). Although the precise sequence of events is difficult to decipher, it appears that Rezin and Pekah lifted the siege of Jerusalem and withdrew to defend their own capitals. While at Gaza, the Assyrians subjugated the cities of the Philistia region and turned the coastal area just north of Philistia into a province. Tiglath-pileser then backtracked northward and forced the submission of Hiram of Tyre. Heading east from Tyre, the Assyrians swept across Galilee, which was probably under Aramean control at this time, and captured cities and prisoners.[52]

By about 733, Damascus and Samaria stood isolated. Tiglath-pileser engaged Damascus for two years, initially defeating Rezin's army in the field and pushing them back into the city. The Assyrians then destroyed outlying cities and territories before eventually sacking Damascus by 731:

I captured his [Rezin's] warriors, archers, shield- and lance-bearers; and I dispersed their battle array. That one [i.e. Rezin], in order to save his life, fled alone; and he entered the gate of his city [like] a mongoose. I impaled alive his chief ministers; and I made his country behold [them]. I set up my camp around the city for 45 days; and I confined him like a bird in a cage... I destroyed 591 cities of 16 districts of Damascus like mounds of ruins after the Deluge.[53]

Rezin was eventually executed and Syrian territory was annexed as a province.

Although Tiglath-pileser claims to have deported some Israelites, he specifically states that he never attacked Samaria: "[A]ll [of whose] cities I leveled ... and I

spared only (isolated) Samaria."[54] Before departing the area in 731 to deal with a situation in Babylon, the Assyrian king established new political boundaries for the west. He appointed Hoshea, a man of unknown origins, who was perhaps already leading an overthrow movement against Pekah, as the new King of Israel, and left him to reclaim Samaria. Assyrian texts testify that the Israelites overthrew Pekah themselves, and biblical texts suggest that Hoshea led a joint Israelite and Judean force up from Judah, perhaps along the same road that Rezin and Pekah had traveled earlier, to recapture Samaria.[55] Upon success, Hoshea sent vassal tribute to the Assyrian king on campaign in southern Babylon. Thus, Israel returned to being an Assyrian vassal kingdom, probably with Judah once again a lesser partner.

Depiction of the Assyrian siege of an unidentified city. The city has a moat (on left), lower wall, and main wall. The left-hand side depicts soldiers using a ladder to scale the city wall and the bottom portion shows the execution of captured inhabitants or soldiers. (Werner Forman Archive)

The events surrounding the Syro-Ephraimitic War reestablished Assyria's dominance over the kingdoms and commerce of Syria-Palestine, and dramatically altered the balance of power. All areas previously controlled by Aram-Damascus, including those in formerly Israelite territory such as Galilee and the northern and central Transjordan, were changed into provinces ruled by Assyrian governors and garrisons. Israel and Judah survived as kingdoms but with greatly reduced borders, probably left holding only those areas west of the Jordan and south of the Jezreel Valley.

Israel and Assyria (730–720 BC)

Tiglath-pileser died on campaign in December 727. Either just before or immediately upon his death, rebellion broke out in the west led by the city of Tyre, and his son and successor Shalmaneser V extended his father's campaign in that direction.

However, the sources for this period are particularly difficult to unravel. There are large gaps and contradictions in the Assyrian records, and the biblical texts condense multiple and complex events into a succinct theological explanation that attributes the fall of Israel to divine punishment for the abandonment of Yahweh and the worship of other gods. All that seems certain is that Israel and Assyria had a protracted period of hostile interaction from 730–720 that included revolts in Samaria and ultimately resulted in the destruction of the northern kingdom by 720. Within this general certainty, sources like 2 Kings 17 suggest that a more specific sequence of events possibly unfolded.

Around 727, when Tyre was in open rebellion, Hoshea of Israel joined other regional rulers and withheld tribute from the new Assyrian king, Shalmaneser V. Hoshea, who had been established as a pro-Assyrian vassal, probably saw Tyre's assertion as a chance to escape from the economic burden of tribute payments to Assyria. Even before his official enthronement ceremony, however, Shalmaneser V campaigned into Syria-Palestine and secured the submission of local kingdoms. While the only source for this campaign is a description by the 1st-century AD Jewish historian Josephus, who claims to be quoting an earlier source that is relying on archives from Tyre, Shalmaneser V probably pressed into Syria and Phoenicia enough to compel them to sign vassal treaties with him, and then he immediately withdrew. Hoshea thus became the new king's vassal and paid tribute in 727.[56]

When Shalmaneser V spent 726 in Assyria, Hoshea apparently again became involved in rebellion and withheld his annual tribute.[57] Tyre was once again the

> The HB/OT's description of the fall of Israel from 2 Kings 17: 1–6 (NRSV): "In the twelfth year of King Ahaz of Judah, Hoshea son of Elah began to reign in Samaria over Israel… King Shalmaneser of Assyria came up against him; Hoshea became his vassal and paid him tribute. But the King of Assyria found treachery in Hoshea; for he had sent messengers to King So of Egypt, and offered no tribute to the King of Assyria, as he had done year by year; therefore the King of Assyria confined him and imprisoned him. Then the King of Assyria invaded all the land and came to Samaria; for three years he besieged it. In the ninth year of Hoshea the King of Assyria captured Samaria; he carried the Israelites away to Assyria."

ring-leader in the west. A particular feature of this 726 rebellion was Hoshea's appeal for help to Egypt, specifically to a "King So."[58] There is no pharaoh known by this name, but it is likely to be a reference to Tefnakht, ruler of the city of Sais, who had come to control virtually the entire Delta a decade earlier. In response, Shalmaneser V led the Assyrian army into the west by 725 with the primary aim of besieging Tyre. Probably at some point during this campaign, Shalmaneser V captured Samaria and imprisoned Hoshea.[59] The Babylonian Chronicle, for example, says Shalmaneser V ravaged Samaria, a reference that may belong to this campaign. It is likely that with the removal of its king in 725, Israel was annexed and turned into the Assyrian province of "Samaria."

About a year later, however, Samaria evidently rebelled again. The HB/OT's notion of a three-year siege against Samaria by Shalmaneser V may represent the Assyrian response.[60] The siege probably began before September/October 724 and ended by December 722. Since Samaria at the time was apparently an Assyrian province without a king, the citizens may have overthrown

King Sargon II of Assyria, who destroyed the Israelite capital of Samaria in 720 BC, and inflicted losses on Judean territory after a failed revolt in 714–711 BC. (akg-images/Erich Lessing)

their Assyrian governor and installed a native king whose name has not survived. The prophet Hosea, for example, offered a message from the god Yahweh that proclaimed, "They carried out a coronation, but not through me."[61] In any case, the Assyrians resubjugated Samaria by 722 but seemingly left the city intact.

Finally, Shalmaneser V died in 722, and Assyria was racked by conflict over the throne; rebellion took root across the Empire. In the west, a coalition of rebellious states formed under the leadership of Yaubi'di of Hamath, involving kingdoms such as Gaza and provinces such as Arpad and Damascus. Assyrian texts explicitly name Samaria as a rebel and refer to the leadership of an unnamed hostile king, perhaps another native ruler enthroned by the citizens for the purpose of revolt.

Sargon II eventually emerged from outside the royal line and usurped the throne of Assyria after suppressing an uprising from sections of the military. He came west late in 720. The ringleader Yaubi'di tried to halt the Assyrians' approach to Syria-Palestine, but Sargon defeated him at the familiar battleground of Qarqar. Pictorial reliefs from Sargon's reign show Yaubi'di being flayed alive after his capture. The Assyrians then moved down the Mediterranean coast to Gaza.

At this point, Sargon encountered in 720 what Tiglath-pileser had feared in 734. After conquering Gaza, Sargon had to push his troops south to meet an advancing Ethiopian force at Raphia, just above the Wadi el-'Arish. Assyrian reliefs show Ethiopian soldiers, typically beardless and curly-haired, fighting against the Assyrians in various cities of southwest Syria-Palestine. The Assyrians defeated the Ethiopians, however, and Sargon claims to have plundered thousands of people and burned Raphia: "I razed, destroyed, and burned Raphia. I carried off 9,033 inhabitants together with their great property."[62]

With the coast secure, Sargon moved against Samaria. Assyrian records do not describe a prolonged siege of the city. Since the other major coalition members had already been defeated, it is likely that Samaria offered little resistance. In any case, Sargon finally secured lasting provincial status for Samaria in 720. He claims to have established an Assyrian governor, classified the people as Assyrian citizens, and incorporated the remaining elements of the military into the Assyrian army. He also deported over 27,000 people and resettled foreigners into the area:

I besieged and conquered Samarina. I took as booty 27,290 people who lived there. I gathered 50 chariots from them… I set my eunuch over them, and I imposed upon them the [same] tribute as the previous king [i.e. Shalmaneser V].[63]

Thus, by the year 720, Sargon controlled the trade and commerce throughout Syria-Palestine. At this time, he also initiated a trade relationship with the Egyptian rulers in the Delta and established a policy of cooperation between Assyria and the

Delta Egyptians (against the Ethiopians) that would last until the end of the Assyrian Empire.

In Judah, King Hezekiah had inherited the throne from his father, Ahaz, around 727. He apparently did not follow Israel in becoming involved in the rebellions against Assyria throughout the 720s. Only one inscription of Sargon mentions subduing Judah, "which is far away." The text probably dates from 720 or 717 but seems to indicate only the renewal of Judean loyalty and not rebellion. It is even possible that Judah in 720 followed the typical protocol for Assyrian vassals illustrated in Assyrian inscriptions, and contributed forces to the Assyrian army in its campaign against Israel.

Judah and Assyria (714–701 BC)

Assyrian kings frequently rewarded kingdoms that remained loyal in the midst of nearby rebellions by giving them expanded territory taken from rebels. Perhaps as a result of its loyalty in 720, Judah experienced a period of political prominence and territorial expansion over the next six years (720–714). This expansion probably involved the influx of refugees from the destroyed northern kingdom, but may also have been tied to Sargon's establishment of trade between Assyria and Egypt. Sargon claims to have reopened a trading post near Egypt, perhaps in Gaza, at the close of the 720 campaign. Second Kings 18: 8 says that around the same time Hezekiah expanded Judean control into the vicinity of Gaza. It is possible that Sargon pushed his territory's border with Egypt south to the Wadi el-'Arish and appointed Hezekiah to supervise the southwest corner of the Empire from 720–714.

After this period of expansion, however, Judah would rebel against Assyria on two occasions: 714–711 and 705–701. When Sargon became occupied in Urartu in 714–713, the people of the Philistine city of Ashdod overthrew their king, whom Sargon had appointed to quell a rebellion two years

earlier, and placed a usurper named Yamani on the throne. He promptly organized a major revolt against Assyrian domination in the west that included other Philistine territories, Edom, and Moab. Assyrian records also list Judah as a participant but do not explicitly name Hezekiah. The inspiration for this revolt came from Egypt, where the new Ethiopian pharaoh Shabako had succeeded the aged Piye and invaded the Delta in 715, and from Babylon, where Merodach-baladan, who had seized the throne in 721, opened hostilities with Assyria in the east. The Assyrian reaction came in 712 or 711. Sargon led his own personal forces, rather than the main army, down the Mediterranean coast and captured Ashdod. Yamani fled to the Ethiopian king Shabako for asylum, and the other rebels capitulated. No siege of Jerusalem is recorded, and Hezekiah remained on the throne.

Given the fact that Hezekiah had remained loyal to Assyria for more than a decade, it is difficult to understand why and how he would have become involved in this rebellion. The HB/OT does not address those issues. The only thing that can be said with certainty is that, for whatever reason, Judah rebelled against Assyria around 714. The biblical and extra-biblical sources allow, however, the following hypothetical sequence of events. The biblical story of Hezekiah suffering a life-threatening illness, which 2 Kings 20 associates with an Assyrian invasion later in Hezekiah's reign, perhaps belongs here, implying that around 714 Hezekiah became incapacitated and turned control of the government over to two officials who subsequently led Judah into the revolt. These two officials are condemned by the prophet Isaiah in a text that is placed in the context of the Ashdod revolt.[64] At the end of the revolt in 712 or 711, Judah apparently suffered some losses. The Assyrians despoiled the Judean stronghold of Azekah and took away Philistine territory that had been under Hezekiah's control. Because he was not personally responsible for the revolt,

Hezekiah survived. Perhaps he recovered from his illness in time to surrender without losing Jerusalem, but Hezekiah probably lost the enhanced status he had between 720 and 714.

The second Judean rebellion against Assyria began about 10 years later. In 705, while fighting a tribal group in the north, Sargon died on the battlefield and revolt broke out across the Empire. In the west, several kingdoms united in rebellion, and this time Assyrian texts specify Hezekiah of Judah as the ringleader. His allies included Sidon, Ashkelon, Ekron, Ammon, Moab, and Edom, and the coalition probably hoped for support from Shebitku, the new king of Ethiopia. Sargon's son, Sennacherib, apparently the third heir born to Sargon but the first to survive childhood, struggled to secure the kingdom, and four years passed before he could campaign in the west.

One possible motivation Hezekiah may have had for rebellion was indignation over having suffered in 711 for a rebellion that he did not initiate, particularly his being deprived of territory in southwestern Judah and the destruction of the city of Azekah. Perhaps as early as 711 or at least by 705, Hezekiah apparently undertook a series of preparations for rebellion and defense that are evidenced in texts and archeology. In Jerusalem, he strengthened the city wall and placed new towers upon it. He also erected a fortification wall, approximately 20ft (6m) thick, to enclose part of the western hill of Jerusalem. Workers dug the so-called "Siloam Tunnel," an underground conduit one-third of a mile long that brought water from the Gihon Spring in the Kidron Valley into the enclosed western side of the city.

Elsewhere, Hezekiah strengthened and reorganized the military, forging new shields and weapons, and inaugurated a royal storage and supply system to send provisions to cities throughout the kingdom. This system consisted of the use of four-handled storage jars, each stamped with an emblem, the Hebrew letters *lmlk* (which were used to signify "for the king"), and the name of one of four regional supply cities from which the stores probably originated. Most of these *lmlk* jars were discovered in the areas of northern

The remains of the additional wall built by King Hezekiah at Jerusalem in the late 8th century BC. The wall was 23ft (7m) wide and served to enclose previously unprotected areas of the city, perhaps in preparation for a revolt against Assyria. (Image courtesy of www.HolyLandPhotos.org)

The "Siloam Tunnel" built by King Hezekiah of Judah in the late 8th century to strengthen Jerusalem against enemy siege. A Hebrew inscription describing construction was found on an inside wall. The tunnel is one-third of a mile long, and brings water from the Gihon Spring in the Kidron Valley outside the city, into a collection pool within the city. (Y Kinory/Ancient Art and Architecture Collection Ltd)

Jerusalem and the Shephelah that would be on the front lines of defense, but some even appeared in the Philistine cities of Ekron and Gath. Biblical texts also attribute a major religious reform to Hezekiah that required the centralizing of Judean worship in Jerusalem by declaring all other sacrificial sites and priestly offices illegitimate. This requirement had the obvious political effect of increasing the power of the capital city.[65]

Sennacherib's campaign to put down the rebellion in 701 is the best-documented event in Judean history, but the sources differ and do not permit certainty in the details. Even so, the combination of the sources suggests Sennacherib followed the well-trodden path of campaigning down the Mediterranean coast and conquered the Phoenician city of Sidon before pressing south to Philistia, where he

met his first major opposition. The Assyrians sacked Ashkelon and Ekron and received the voluntary capitulation of other rebels like Edom, Moab, and Ammon. At this point, Sennacherib seems to have confronted a combined Egyptian and Ethiopian force that had marched up from Egypt to Eltekeh in the Philistine territory west of Jerusalem. This was a force of the Ethiopian Shebitku, who was also in control of the Delta, and may have been under the command of the crown prince Tirhakah (Taharqa) mentioned in 2 Kings 19: 9, "When the king [Sennacherib] heard concerning King Tirhakah of Ethiopia, 'See, he has set out to fight against you...'"[66]

By defeating this Egyptian force, the Assyrians secured the major areas leading eastward into Judean territory. Sennacherib then invaded southwestern Judah. Archeological evidence of destruction is present at cities like Ramet Rahel, Beth-Shemesh, Beersheba, and Gezer. The Assyrians claim to have captured 46 cities and exiled 200,150 people, although this number seems too large for the geographical area. The siege and capture of Lachish was the most significant accomplishment of the

Sennacherib's campaign against Judah 701 BC

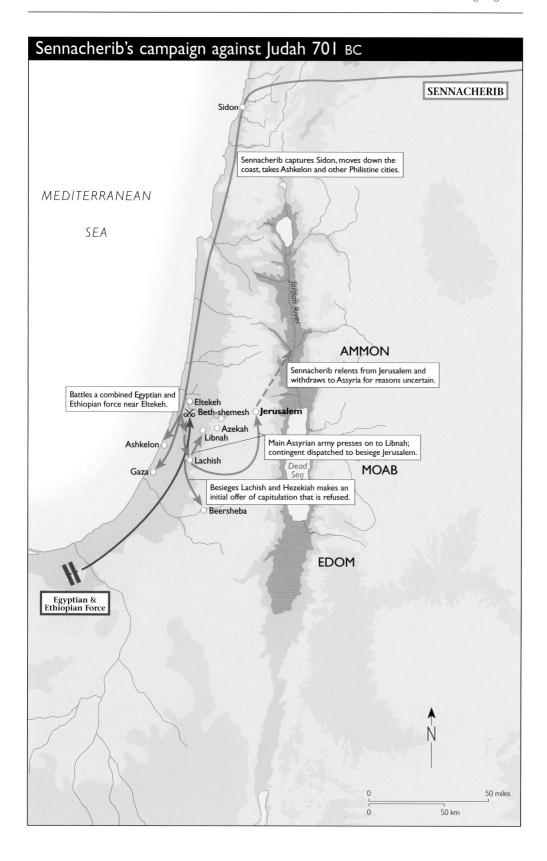

SENNACHERIB

MEDITERRANEAN

SEA

Sidon

Sennacherib captures Sidon, moves down the coast, takes Ashkelon and other Philistine cities.

Jordan River

AMMON

Sennacherib relents from Jerusalem and withdraws to Assyria for reasons uncertain.

Battles a combined Egyptian and Ethiopian force near Eltekeh.

Eltekeh
Beth-shemesh   Jerusalem
Azekah
Libnah

Ashkelon

Main Assyrian army presses on to Libnah; contingent dispatched to besiege Jerusalem.

Gaza

Lachish

Dead Sea

MOAB

Besieges Lachish and Hezekiah makes an initial offer of capitulation that is refused.

Beersheba

EDOM

Egyptian & Ethiopian Force

N

0   50 miles
0   50 km

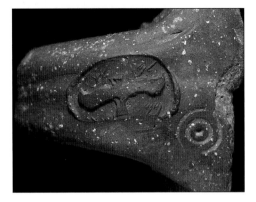

TOP 8th-century BC storage jars found at Lachish, inscribed with the phrase, "belonging to the king," or *lmlk*. The jars, also found at other cities in Judah and Philistia, probably formed part of a supply network instituted by King Hezekiah in anticipation of an Assyrian invasion around 701 BC. (British Museum, London)

BOTTOM Close-up of an 8th-century Judean storage jar from the time of Hezekiah that shows the stamp of a winged emblem, as well as a Hebrew inscription, *lmlk*. (British Museum, London)

campaign, since it was a heavily fortified city controlling access to southwestern Judah. A wall relief in Sennacherib's palace in Nineveh commemorated the battle for Lachish and depicted Assyrian siege machinery and troops, as well as Israelite soldiers defending the city with arrows, stones, and torches.

The available sources favor the conclusion that while the Assyrian army was at Lachish, Hezekiah made an initial offer of capitulation that did not include the surrender of Jerusalem: "King Hezekiah of Judah sent to the king of Assyria at Lachish, saying, 'I have done wrong; withdraw from me; whatever you impose on me I will bear.'"[67] Sennacherib apparently refused this offer and dispatched a contingent of soldiers led by the "Rabshakeh," an Assyrian diplomatic spokesperson, to place Jerusalem under siege and force its surrender.[68] The Assyrians built either a siege wall of earthwork around the city or a series of blockades/outposts to control all incoming and outgoing traffic. Second Kings 18–19[69] may contain the actual speech of the Rabshakeh, who used political and religious rhetoric to call the city to surrender:

Do not let Hezekiah deceive you, for he will not be able to deliver you out of my hand. Do not let Hezekiah make you rely on the LORD by saying, The LORD will surely deliver us… Has any of the gods of the nations ever delivered its land out of the hand of the king of Assyria … that the LORD should deliver Jerusalem out of my hand?[70]

Ultimately, the sources agree that Jerusalem was never taken, Hezekiah remained on the throne, and Sennacherib returned home to Nineveh. In Sennacherib's account, he states:

He [Hezekiah] *himself, I locked up within Jerusalem, his royal city, like a bird in a cage. I surrounded him with earthworks, and made it unthinkable for him to exit by the city gate. His cities which I had despoiled I cut off from his land and gave them to Mitini, king of Ashdod, Padi, king of Ekron and Silli-bel, king of Gaza, and thus diminished his land. I imposed dues and gifts for my lordship upon him, in addition to the former tribute, their yearly payment. He, Hezekiah … sent me after my departure to Nineveh, my royal city, his elite troops (and) his best soldiers, which he had brought in as reinforcements to strengthen Jerusalem, with 30 talents of gold* [and other tribute].[71]

There are, however, differing traditions about what precipitated this conclusion.

Biblical texts attribute this to the miraculous overnight slaying of 185,000 Assyrian soldiers by an angel, a tradition that is similar to a later Greek story about a miraculous defeat of Sennacherib in Egypt. Assyrian records indicate that Hezekiah sent a very large tribute to Nineveh and suffered substantial devastation of wider Judean territory. Perhaps news of trouble back home reached Sennacherib and thus he allowed Hezekiah to capitulate without losing Jerusalem. In all likelihood, Sennacherib stationed a garrison at Lachish to maintain future control of the area. In the end, Sennacherib did not turn any of the rebellious kingdoms into provinces in 701, a move in keeping with Assyria's policy of retaining seaport and southern kingdoms, as opposed to northern and central kingdoms, as semi-independent vassals and thereby buffers with Egypt.

Nabopolassar was the founder of the "Neo-Babylonian Empire" that wrested control of the Ancient Near East away from Assyria beginning in 626 BC. His origins are unclear, but later Greek historians suggested he served one of the last Assyrian kings before leading a rebellion in the city of Babylon. He may have been Chaldean from southern Babylonia in ethnicity.

A rendering of the possible appearance of the ancient Judean city of Lachish before its destruction by the Assyrians in 701 BC. Assyrian texts and archeological remains attest to the presence of double walls, fortified towers, and a large central building complex. (British Museum, London)

Judah and Babylonia (597–586 BC)

Hezekiah's failed revolt inaugurated a long period in which Judah was a submissive vassal while Assyria reached the pinnacle of its power (698–627). The rise of Nabopolassar in Babylonia in 626, however, marked the beginning of Assyria's downfall. At the time of his rise, groups of semi-nomads, especially the Medes from the northwest region of modern Iran, began to move into Assyrian territory. By 612, the Babylonians and Medes had formed an alliance and captured the Assyrian religious center of Ashur, as well as the administrative capital of Nineveh.

During this period (626–612), Egypt under Psammetichus I sided with Assyria against the Babylonians and Medes. The Egyptians must have concluded that their interests were best served by continuing their economic and power-sharing arrangements with the empire they had known for more than a century. At the time of Assyria's demise and gradual withdrawal from the west, evidence suggests that Egypt captured

Part of the relief from Sennacherib's palace in Nineveh that pictures the Assyrian siege of Lachish in 701 BC. The picture shows Judean archers fighting from a tower, men and women exiting the city with their goods, and three men impaled outside the city. (British Museum, London)

Ashdod, established military outposts at cities like Riblah, Carchemish, and Haran, and controlled the main north–south route on the seaboard. This Egyptian dominance had an impact on affairs in Judah under Hezekiah's great-grandson, King Josiah (641–610). Despite the impression of independence given to him by the biblical writers,[72] he may have been subservient, perhaps even as a vassal, to Egypt during the majority of his reign.

When Nineveh fell to the Babylonians and Medes in 612, the remnants of the Assyrian army retreated to Haran, 100 miles (160km) west of Nineveh, probably to be within reach of Egyptian assistance. At this time a new pharaoh, Necho II, marched northward through Syria-Palestine to assist the Assyrians. On the way, for reasons that are unknown, he killed Josiah at Megiddo.[73] Upon Josiah's death, a segment of the Judean people placed his younger son, Jehoahaz II on the throne.

In the fall of 610, the Babylonians and Medes forced the Assyrians and Egyptians to withdraw from Haran. Necho fell back and set up a temporary headquarters at Riblah. In an apparent exercise of his control over Judah, Necho summoned Jehoahaz II to Riblah and imprisoned him there. From June/July through to August/September of 609, the Egyptians and Assyrians counterattacked Haran from the west but were unable to take the city. This battle marked the end of Assyria as a factor in the Ancient Near East. Necho withdrew but maintained nominal control over Syria-Palestine up to the area of Carchemish. On his return south in 609, the pharaoh placed Jehoahaz II's older brother, Jehoiakim on the throne in Jerusalem as an Egyptian vassal.

The turning point for all of Syria-Palestine came a few years later with the battle of Carchemish in the summer of 605, the major

In this scene from the relief in Sennacherib's palace in Nineveh showing the Assyrian siege of Lachish (701 BC), Assyrian soldiers lead away two Judean captives, perhaps royal officials, who hold their hands in the posture of a plea for leniency. (Werner Forman Archive)

contest for western dominance between the remaining powers of Egypt and Babylonia. The Babylonians were led by the Crown Prince Nebuchadrezzar II. Babylonian texts suggest that they did not initially attempt a direct assault on Carchemish, but spent the two years before 605 isolating the city by driving a wedge southward across northern Syria. In April of 605, however, the Babylonians surprised the Egyptians with a direct assault on Carchemish from the south. The Egyptian army withdrew to Egypt and left Syria-Palestine open for the Babylonians.

During the following period of 605–603, Nebuchadrezzar, who had now ascended the throne in Babylon, marched throughout Syria-Palestine establishing vassal kingdoms, and Jehoiakim officially switched Judah's loyalty from Egypt to Babylonia. Babylonian policy at this time was evidently to leave the local administrations that they encountered in place; hence, Jehoiakim was left on the throne even though he had been an Egyptian appointee.

The Babylonians apparently decided that they could not allow Egypt to remain independent. Thus, in late 601, Nebuchadrezzar invaded Egypt but was defeated by Necho. When Nebuchadrezzar spent the next year in Babylon rebuilding his chariot forces, Necho advanced northward into Syria-Palestine, possibly conquering Gaza.[74] Perhaps envisioning a resurgence of Egypt, Jehoiakim withheld tribute in rebellion against Babylonia around 600 or 599.

The Babylonian response began in late November or early December 598, when Nebuchadrezzar led the main army out of Akkad toward the specific target of Jerusalem. No details of his march or of the siege itself are known. Before his arrival in the west, however, Nebuchadrezzar apparently sent auxiliary forces from the Chaldeans, Arameans, Moabites, and Ammonites into Judean territory, an action that the HB/OT interprets as divine punishment: "The LORD sent against him bands of the Chaldeans, bands of the Arameans, bands of the Moabites, and bands of the Ammonites…"[75] These groups probably captured Judean outposts in the Negeb and caused inhabitants of the outlying territories to flee into Jerusalem.

Although there are differing biblical traditions about what happened to Jehoiakim[76], it appears that he died in office while the Babylonians were still en route to Jerusalem. His 18-year-old son, Jehoiachin, inherited both his father's royal throne and ill-advised rebellion in December 598. Three months later, the Babylonian army arrived in Judah and laid siege to Jerusalem. Evidently Jehoiachin immediately surrendered without resistance, and the Babylonians took control of the city on March 15 or 16, 597:

Year 7 [598–597], *month Kislev* [December–January]: *the king of Akkad moved his army in Hatti land* [west], *laid siege to the city of Judah* [Jerusalem] *and on the second day of the month Adar* [15 or 16 March] *he captured the city and seized its king. He appointed in it a king of his liking, took heavy booty from it and sent it to Babylon.*[77]

Probably because Jehoiachin was not personally responsible for the revolt and offered immediate surrender, Nebuchadrezzar did not destroy Jerusalem or provincialize Judah. He took Jehoiachin, along with his mother, servants, officials, craftsmen, and trained soldiers, into exile. Nebuchadrezzar left the dynasty intact, however, and appointed 21-year-old Zedekiah, Jehoiachin's uncle, to the throne. This lenient move was in keeping with Babylonian policy at the time to avoid disrupting stability and creating vacuums that stronger enemies could fill.

Zedekiah's loyalty to Babylon after 597 was short-lived. The biblical account in 2 Kings 24–25 skips from the beginning to the end of his reign. Other biblical materials

An Assyrian relief that shows soldiers of the Medes, a group from the northwest region of modern Iran that formed an alliance with the Babylonians against the Assyrians in the late 7th century BC. (akg-images/Erich Lessing)

like the prophetic books of Jeremiah and Ezekiel, however, provide more potential information. Sometime shortly after Nebuchadrezzar returned to Babylon in 597, Zedekiah apparently hosted a conference in Jerusalem with officials from Edom, Moab, Ammon, Tyre, and Sidon[78] in order to coordinate a rebellion in the west in concert with Elam and others in the east. Elam initiated hostilities against Babylon in 595 or 594, but the revolt failed. Perhaps in response to these events, Nebuchadrezzar brought Zedekiah to Babylon in 594–593, probably to ensure his loyalty.[79]

After Zedekiah's return to Jerusalem, Pharaoh Psammetichus II, who had come to the Egyptian throne in 595, initiated an aggressive campaign against Ethiopia in 592/591 that resulted in a sweeping Egyptian victory. To celebrate this victory, Psammetichus II embarked on a victory tour of Syria-Palestine in 591. Probably as a result of this Egyptian resurgence, coupled with long-standing Judean religious beliefs in the inviolability of Jerusalem, Zedekiah withheld annual tribute and entered into open rebellion against Babylonia in the late 590s or early 580s. Biblical and extra-biblical texts depict Judah appealing to Egypt for horses and troops and sending royal officials to Egypt for direct negotiations.

During this renewed rebellion in the west, an aggressive new pharaoh, Hophra or Apries, came to the Egyptian throne in 589. The combination of these factors led the Babylonians to change their earlier policy of maintaining stability. Nebuchadrezzar apparently decided henceforth to replace currently ruling families, relocate rebellious kingdoms' centers of power, and rule them more directly. Thus, in the late fall of 589, Nebuchadrezzar set out from Babylonia to make Jerusalem the first example of this new policy. He led his forces to central Syria and established a base of operations at Riblah. There he evidently divided his army and sent one contingent down the coast toward the border of Egypt and another toward Jerusalem where they placed the city under siege in January 587. For his part, Zedekiah's

military tactics included establishing a network of communication among commanders and garrisons at key Judean cities. Messages on *ostraca* (inscribed potsherds) and papyrus were sent from Jerusalem to the commander of a particular location such as Lachish, who then sent them to another post. Within the capital, Zedekiah freed the slaves in order to add new levies for defense.

During the siege of Jerusalem, an Egyptian force of Hophra/Apries was able to break into Syria-Palestine and force the Babylonians to withdraw from the city temporarily. The Egyptians seem to have retreated without a confrontation, however, and the Babylonians reinstated the siege. Near the end of July 586, 18 months after the siege began, the Babylonians breached the city wall in the north or west:

And in the ninth year of his [Zedekiah's] *reign, in the tenth month, on the tenth day of the month, King Nebuchadrezzar of Babylon came with all his army against Jerusalem, and laid siege to it… On the ninth day of the fourth month the famine became so severe in the city that there was no food for the people of the land. Then a breach was made in the city wall…*[80]

Biblical texts add that Zedekiah and a military escort attempted to flee south toward the Transjordan but were captured and brought to Nebuchadrezzar at Riblah. Probably in keeping with the stipulated punishments of his vassal treaty, Zedekiah's sons were killed in front of him, his eyes were put out, and he was sent to Babylonia in chains: "They slaughtered the sons of Zedekiah before his eyes, then put out the eyes of Zedekiah; they bound him in fetters and took him to Babylon."[81]

In keeping with the Babylonians' new western policy, the written sources indicate a severe treatment of Jerusalem. About one month after the city's capture, Nebuchadrezzar sent Nebuzaradan, captain of the royal guard, to raze Jerusalem. He burned the temple, palace, and houses, and broke down the city walls. Biblical

Nebuchadrezzar's campaign against Judah 586 BC

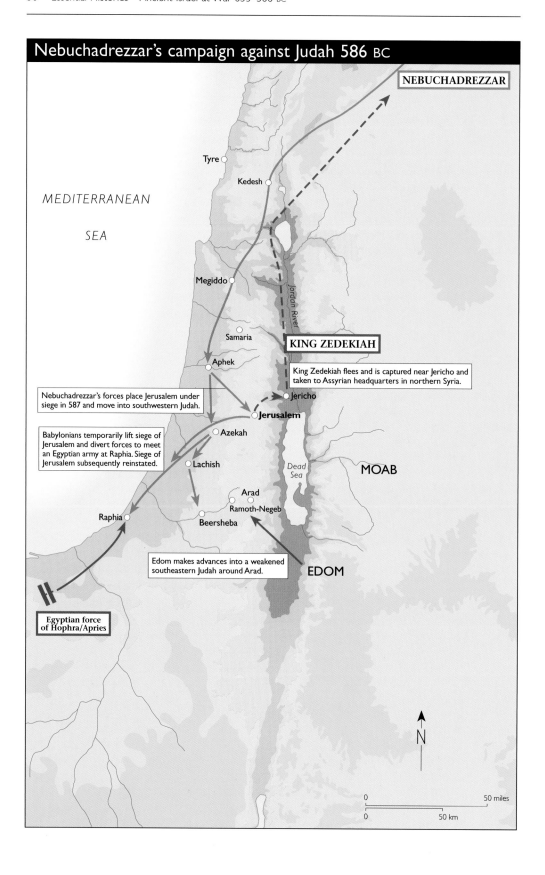

NEBUCHADREZZAR

Tyre

Kedesh

MEDITERRANEAN

SEA

Megiddo

Jordan River

Samaria

KING ZEDEKIAH

Aphek

King Zedekiah flees and is captured near Jericho and taken to Assyrian headquarters in northern Syria.

Nebuchadrezzar's forces place Jerusalem under siege in 587 and move into southwestern Judah.

Jericho

Jerusalem

Azekah

Babylonians temporarily lift siege of Jerusalem and divert forces to meet an Egyptian army at Raphia. Siege of Jerusalem subsequently reinstated.

Lachish

Dead Sea

MOAB

Arad

Ramoth-Negeb

Raphia

Beersheba

Edom makes advances into a weakened southeastern Judah around Arad.

EDOM

Egyptian force of Hophra/Apries

N

| 0 | | 50 miles |
| 0 | | 50 km |

texts contain differing accounts of the deportations that followed,[82] but probably most of the inhabitants of Jerusalem were exiled, as well as about 800 Judeans from surrounding areas. The Babylonians rendered the city of Jerusalem desolate.

The new Babylonian policy apparently did not, however, entail the complete annihilation of rebellious kingdoms but only the removal of the old royal center and family. With the exception of the major military cities of Lachish and Azekah, there is little evidence of destruction outside of Jerusalem, especially in the area directly north. The Babylonians evidently chose this area for a new administrative capital of Judah under a hand-picked leader. With Jerusalem destroyed, the Babylonians then pressed their new policy of removal and reduction toward Sidon, Tyre, Ammon, and Moab.

A reconstructed model of the "Ishtar Gate" of Nebuchadrezzar II at the ancient city of Babylon. (© bpk, Berlin)

Pekah, son of Remaliah: rebel, officer, king

Pekah, son of Remaliah, was arguably the most significant figure in Israel's history during the 8th century BC, and is known to us from both the HB/OT and Assyrian inscriptions. He affected the reigns of five different Israelite kings, and dramatically altered the course of Israelite policy in relation to Aram-Damascus, Judah, and Assyria. Although all reconstructions of ancient persons remain tentative, it seems that during the course of his military career Pekah progressed from a common soldier, to a rebel leader, to a royal officer, to the sole ruler of the northern kingdom. The HB/OT records a few specific pieces of biographical information for him: firstly, before he became king he served as a military officer to the preceding king; secondly, he reigned for 20 years in Israel; thirdly, while he was king, he joined King Rezin of Damascus in an attack on Jerusalem. Pekah's life also provides a glimpse of the experiences of being a soldier in ancient Israel.

The significant part of Pekah's career began around 750 when Rezin of Damascus, who had recently usurped the throne, launched his effort to throw off Assyrian control of the west, and to reestablish Aramean dominance in Syria-Palestine. These actions took place during the final years of the reign of Jeroboam II in Samaria, and the period of the Assyrian Empire's decline in the years just before Tiglath-pileser III assumed the throne. Probably due to his desire to replace Assyrian control, Rezin immediately initiated hostilities against Israel, where the central administration in Samaria had been pro-Assyrian in its foreign policy since the time of Jehu (c.841). While Rezin tried to gain control over the Israelite territories that most directly bordered his own, namely, Gilead in the northern Transjordan and

Galilee north of Samaria and west of the Jordan River, he was probably already working to form a coalition to oppose Assyrian dominance and to reassert the level of regional control that Damascus had possessed under Hazael in the 9th century.

Pekah was an Israelite soldier from Gilead in the Transjordan, who evidently came to sympathize with the anti-Assyrian sentiments of his Aramean neighbor to the north. In this context, we can imagine what experiences he and his fellow soldiers underwent. As a "regular" soldier in the standing army, Pekah may have been a member of a division of 50 or 100 infantrymen under the command of one ranking officer. At times joining with similar divisions and at times operating independently, Pekah's division was probably a mobile infantry group, not stationed in any one town but moving from camp to camp throughout the region, yet having strong local ties to its men's ancestral hometowns in the area. As an infantry group, it almost certainly operated as foot soldiers carrying a spear or javelin, personal shield, and perhaps a sword at their side. Standard dress was probably a short tunic and boots, while battle gear was likely to include scale armor, a breastplate, and perhaps a helmet.[83]

In a tumultuous border region like the Transjordan area of Gilead, a soldier like Pekah was probably involved in continual deployments and redeployments designed to counter Aramean moves into Israelite territory. At times, soldier divisions probably formed reaction forces and mobilized to besiege and retake towns that had fallen under Aramean occupation and plunder. On other occasions, Pekah perhaps found himself temporarily garrisoned in a town in order to fortify it against Aramean

A seal inscribed with the picture and name of "Pekah," who became king in Samaria around 734 BC. The seal, although broken, pictures him striding and wearing a short tunic but without a crown, perhaps suggesting it comes from the time before he ascended the throne. (Vorderasiatische Museum, Berlin)

advancement. It is not difficult to imagine that a border-region native like Pekah would have grown weary of the constant warfare within and destruction of his ancestral territory. To a soldier hailing from and serving in a territory so heavily influenced by the anti-Assyrian efforts of Damascus, the stubborn loyalty of the central Israelite government in Samaria to an Assyrian Empire without any strong presence in the region and the resulting hostilities with Aram-Damascus may have been difficult to support.

Perhaps for this reason, the presentations in later biblical and extra-biblical texts imply that when Rezin finally gained control of Gilead and Galilee, Pekah emerged from the Israelite ranks and was installed as ruler of these areas under Aramean oversight. Thus, Pekah emerged as a rival claimant to the throne in the Kingdom of Israel near the end of the reign of Jeroboam II, and both Assyrian and biblical texts present him as the primary ally of Rezin for the next two decades. He probably represented a significant faction of the Israelite population that saw the Damascus-led anti-Assyrian policy as the proper course for the kingdom at the time.

For the next 15 years after 750, Pekah continued his presence as a rival ruler and fostered further division among the people of Israel over which foreign policy to follow. The HB/OT's assignment of a 20-year reign to Pekah may include these years of divided rule.[84] Because of this division within the kingdom, these years also saw a steady loss of territory and control by the central government in Samaria. Rezin and Pekah even jointly harassed Judah as early as the time of King Jotham (c.750s): "In those days, the LORD began to send King Rezin of Aram and Pekah son of Remaliah against Judah."[85] By the time of Jeroboam's successors, Menahem (746–737) and his son Pekahiah (736–735), the king who sat in Samaria probably had firm control of only the capital city and its immediate vicinity, with Pekah holding Galilee and Gilead.

We cannot be certain about what happened next, but when Pekahiah succeeded his father Menahem to the Israelite throne in 736, Pekah's status may have changed. It was possibly at this point that King Pekahiah established Pekah as a *shalish* ("officer", "captain") within his military administration, which is how the HB/OT remembers Pekah.[86] This move would appear to have been an attempt to reunify the government and regain lost territory that was under Pekah's rule or influence. At times, the rank of *shalish* designated a personal assistant to the king,[87] but Pekah's experience as a "captain" was more likely as a member of a group of commanding officers or elite warriors within the military organization.[88] The office shared some of the functions of and perhaps developed out of the older position of the *nose' kelim* ("armor-bearer"), which had been prominent in Israel during the early stages of military development before the 9th century. An armor-bearer was a personal attendant or group of attendants who kept the equipment of a warrior, and also accompanied him into battle, often being charged with finishing off enemies who had been mortally wounded.[89] It perhaps gave way to the broader *shalish* office when the Israelite military became increasingly centralized around the monarchy, beginning in the 10th century.

Given the long-standing history of Pekah's rebellious activity, however, it is likely that he served only as one member among Pekahiah's group of "captains," rather than as a personal attendant of the king. A possible representation of Pekah in this capacity appears on an 8th-century seal found in the Samaria region. The seal, which was used to affix personal identifications to correspondence, bears the Hebrew name Pekah and pictures a striding figure with a wig, a short tunic, and a javelin in an upraised right hand. If the representation is Pekah, it shows him without a crown and is thus similar to the seals of other officers but not those of kings.

Pekah did not last in the role of Pekahiah's captain, however. Around 735, when the Assyrians withdrew from the west after having conquered Hamath in northern Syria, and Rezin's coalition entered into open rebellion against Assyria, Pekah made his move on the throne in Samaria. As the HB/OT indicates, sometime between September and November 734, Pekah led a contingent of 50 men from Gilead into Samaria, assassinated Pekahiah in the palace citadel, and usurped control of the entire northern kingdom:

Pekah son of Remaliah, his [Pekahiah's] captain, conspired against him with fifty of the Gileadites, and attacked him in Samaria, in the citadel of the palace along with Argob and Arieh; he killed him, and reigned in place of him.[90]

His coup was both an internal palace revolt by a royal officer, and the product of rebel groups in particular areas that were sympathetic to Rezin's anti-Assyrian movement.

For over a century, Pekah's royal predecessors in Samaria had successfully maintained at least powerful influence if not control over the southern kingdom. But, as noted in the last chapter, upon Pekah's usurpation the Judean king, Ahaz, asserted his independence. He refused to join the anti-Assyrian coalition, so Rezin and Pekah led a coalition force south from Samaria and laid siege to Jerusalem shortly after Pekah's coup: "Then King Rezin of Aram and King Pekah son of Remaliah of Israel came up to wage war on Jerusalem; they besieged Ahaz but could not conquer him."[91] Seen more specifically from Pekah's perspective, this siege was not simply about establishing a unified front against Assyria, but was an attempt to resubjugate Judah and gain a level of authority equal to those who had gone before him. Another biblical tradition expands Pekah's personal involvement in these events by claiming that he killed 120,000 Judean warriors in a single day:

Pekah son of Remaliah killed one hundred and twenty thousand in Judah in one day, all of them valiant warriors, because they had abandoned the LORD, the God of their ancestors.[92]

When Tiglath-pileser III led the Assyrian army down the Mediterranean coast in late 734, Pekah withdrew from Jerusalem, separated from Rezin, and retreated into his capital at Samaria. He would never again leave the city. As the Assyrians systematically subdued the members of the coalition and killed Rezin, a pro-Assyrian overthrow movement apparently formed within Israel. Prophets began to describe Pekah and his capital as a promiscuous woman and sickening wound and to declare that it was God's will to bring destruction upon them:

Plead with your mother [Samaria?], plead … that she put away her whoring from her face, and her adultery from between her breasts… When Ephraim saw his sickness, and Judah his wound, then Ephraim went to Assyria, and sent to the great king.[93]

In this atmosphere, Tiglath-pileser did not need to attack Samaria. While Pekah remained barricaded in his capital, Tiglath-pileser designated Hoshea, a previously unknown figure who was perhaps the leader of the overthrow movement, as the new ruler of Israel, probably returning Judah to Israel's control, and departed the region in early summer 731: "[They killed] Pekah, their king, and I installed Hoshea [as king] over them."[94]

Exactly when and how Pekah met his end is unknown. He was probably able to hold out in Samaria until around October or November 731, but was eventually deposed and killed by Hoshea: "Then Hoshea son of Elah made a conspiracy against Pekah son of Remaliah, attacked him, and killed him."[95] Pekah had succeeded, however, in introducing the sentiments of rebellion against, and freedom from, Assyria that would surface repeatedly throughout the reign of his assassin and ultimately result in Israel's destruction by 720.

The effects of conflict

From the 9th to the 6th century BC, periods of prolonged conflict were the norm for Israel and Judah; years of peace and stability were merely interludes in a progression of wars. The elements that accompanied these conflicts – the development of alliances established by commercial trade, the need for military personnel and materials, and the enemy incursions into and destructions within the kingdoms – significantly affected their socio-economic structures and religious belief systems.

Society and economy

Throughout the period of the monarchies in Israel and Judah, both kingdoms existed as agrarian societies that were primarily dependent upon plant cultivation and animal husbandry for survival. Even though there were significant cities like Samaria and Jerusalem, a great deal of the population lived in small farming villages of 100–250 people. In the period prior to the outbreak of major military conflicts in the mid-9th century, evidence from texts and archeology suggests that these villages revolved around a family-based mode of production in which family units cooperated to share labor and distribute the risk of crop failure. In this subsistence economy, the farmers kept the majority of their surplus resources in order to provide for their own survival. While there was no private ownership of land in the modern sense, family units maintained plots of land that were passed on through inheritance.

This agrarian society also operated on a patron–client system: certain local leaders who had access to goods and the centers of power ("patrons") entered into cooperative relationships with the local farmers and producers ("clients"). Prior to the mid-9th century, this patronage relationship was reciprocal between the ruling and producing groups. After meeting their own needs, the villages provided a portion of their surplus to a local leader who had limited power. He depended upon the farmers for goods and labor, and they depended upon him for protection and support.

The major military conflicts between 853 and 586, however, brought about changes in the social and economic structures. These changes were often the result of political alliances established through commercial trade, increased need for Israel and Judah to "stock up" on military personnel, materials, and buildings, and the oppression of Israel and Judah by kingdoms like Aram-Damascus, Assyria, and Babylonia. Such wartime developments began to shift the socio-economic structures of Israel and Judah toward oppression, inequality, and poverty, especially for the farmers/producers. The economy gradually changed from a family-based subsistence economy to a centralized economy in which the royal administration dictated the distribution of resources according to the demands of interregional trade and foreign domination. The forging of offensive and defensive alliances, for example, produced profits from imports and exports and allowed for some prosperity. The central administration, however, distributed these profits to the local rulers (patrons). Rather than allowing the goods to "trickle down" to the village farmers, the rulers acquired luxury items like ivory for themselves while continuing to drain the surplus of the villages. This practice increasingly denied farmers the resources needed to sustain production.

The central government also practiced land consolidation by giving land grants to military and administrative functionaries

An olive press. Such facilities were used to support the increased royal demands for wine and oil throughout the periods of Israel's major wars. (akg-images/Erich Lessing)

and establishing large estates controlled by wealthy elites. Thus, a new urban elite class displaced family-based village structures. The ancestral lands of peasant farmers were increasingly subsumed into the boundaries of royally designated estates. The farmers probably had to pay rent or taxes on the lands they worked, and in bad years they may have had to surrender any claim to the lands in order to gain the seed needed to plant for survival. Some villagers may even have found themselves working like tenant farmers on the very lands that had been in their families for generations. This economic strain also must have forced some members of farming families into military service. Many villagers' lands and inheritance were now probably insufficient to provide for male children other than the firstborn heir. With little other recourse for survival, many of these younger sons probably joined – voluntarily or otherwise – the military.

As Israel and Judah continued to engage in political alliances and military conflicts, the demand for military resources increased. Thus, goods that could have provided for the needs of peasants had to be increasingly used to purchase materials for fortified palaces and city walls or to provide stores and supplies for soldiers. The capital city's increased need for these materials also required the local and regional royal functionaries to give up more of their share of the economic resources and threatened the prosperity they had previously known. In order to maintain this prosperity, these rulers shifted the burden to the farmers/producers, probably through increased rent payments and higher production demands.

The economic strain increased as Israel and Judah became subject to foreign powers. The village farmers lost not only resources because of the need to supply the military, but also because of the need to pay the required tributes to ruling empires. In order to meet these two demands, the kingdoms needed to produce particular commodities that were easily gathered, stored, and transported. Biblical and archeological indicators suggest that these commodities were especially grain, oil, and wine. Hence, the royal administration engaged in a process of imposed "cash cropping." The rulers forced farmers and villages to transform their lands into vineyards and olive orchards and to produce only the specialized cash crops of grain, wine, and oil for use by the central government. Specialization of oil and wine

Remains of a "casemate" wall from the northern Israelite city of Hazor. These structures consisted of two parallel walls with the space between them divided into smaller compartments, and served to bolster the defenses of a city. (Ronald Sheridan, Ancient Art and Architecture Collection Ltd)

production was especially prevalent in the hill country, while the intensified grain production was centered in the lowland areas. Archeological remains show, for example, the multiplication of rock-cut olive and grape processing stations around Samaria in the 8th century. About 65 notations written on potsherds, which date from the 9th/8th centuries and were found in a storehouse in Samaria, also register the delivery of olive oil and wine and may be records of the receipt of such items from royal estates outside of the capital.

The effects of this cash cropping on the village farmers were devastating. Under pressure to grow only specialized crops, the farmers lost their ability to raise what they needed for local subsistence. Many peasants had to take out loans from the ruling elite who had control of basic subsistence resources granted by the central government. To get

these loans, the farmers offered their inherited lands, family members, or even their own persons as collateral. When the almost inevitable foreclosures occurred, peasants frequently became landless debt-slaves to members of the ruling elite. Various biblical texts suggest that even the courts of law charged with supervising such loans and foreclosures increasingly came to be controlled by the ruling elites, and thus came to be corrupted to serve their interests. Farmers also lost the ability to use agricultural practices like crop rotation and fallowing to spread risks of crop failure. Instead, they had to invest time, labor, and resources into establishing terrace-farming of vineyards and olive trees and engage in continuous sowing and reaping in order to support the royal land agenda.

Religion

War fundamentally affected Israelite and Judean religion. Religious beliefs and practices became avenues by which the royal houses legitimized their policies and others opposed them.

The official dynasty-sponsored religion throughout the 9th to 6th centuries centered on the worship of the god Yahweh, and was expressed through the practice of priests and sacrifices. This worship was "monolatrous," that is, it promoted the exclusive worship of Yahweh without denying the existence of other deities. The HB/OT is an extensive source for these religious beliefs and practices. While the Bible is evidently not a historical annal, it is explicitly a collection of ancient Israelite and Judean religious texts. These texts, as well as evidence from extra-biblical writings and archeology, show that the official religion was not static, uniform, or universal throughout households in Israel and Judah, and that the various wars helped to shape the official religion in diverse ways.

One strand of Israelite religion came to see the god Yahweh as a "divine warrior" who fought alongside Israel's troops and provided the decisive factor in their victories. This belief appears in some of the most ancient poems preserved in the HB/OT and may have had its roots in Israel's pre-monarchical period. Especially in Israel's struggles against stronger and dominating empires, the Israelites came to see Yahweh as a warrior who acted in violent ways on behalf of the weaker group in order to provide deliverance from oppression and security for existence:

The LORD is a warrior; the LORD is his name... Your right hand, O LORD, glorious in power – your right hand, O LORD, shattered the enemy;[96] *The LORD your God, who goes before you, is the one who will fight for you... Do not fear them, for it is the LORD your God who fights for you.*[97]

Such a belief was also similar to what other Ancient Near Eastern kingdoms said about their gods. By casting their own historical battles as events in which God was involved, the Israelites transformed those battles into larger conflicts between their God and cosmic forces of evil represented by other gods. Even so, biblical texts insisted that Yahweh's first loyalty was to justice and righteousness and that he was not unconditionally loyal to Israel, a concession that probably helped explain defeats suffered in battle.

The king and his royal officials, who sought to maintain the social and economic structures they had instituted, used such beliefs to give themselves moral and religious legitimacy. Amidst the military conflicts led by the king and capital, Israel's religion developed a "royal theology" that pictured God as siding with the king against all enemies of the kingdom, and envisioned the king himself as the human representative of the divine warrior. This theology appeared in several ancient royal hymns that have been preserved in the biblical book of Psalms and that simultaneously honor both the rule of God and the rule of the king:

Then he [Yahweh] will speak to them in his wrath..."I have set my king on Zion, my holy hill... Ask of me, and I will make the nations your heritage, and the ends of the earth your possession. You shall break them with a rod of iron, and dash them in pieces like a potter's vessel."[98]

By making an explicit connection between the divine warrior and the royal establishment, this belief system legitimated the monarchy's policies and the socio-economic order that they produced. Under this system, the elements of religious practice often became intertwined with the government's interests. Royal sanctuaries at places like Bethel and Jerusalem functioned as administrative and economic centers, and priests in local areas promoted the dominant religious ideology and managed economic resources. Sacrifices and offerings given by the people served as sources of revenue for the government, since only a portion of the offering was consumed on the altar and the remainder went to the priest for redistribution or re-use.[99]

At times, Israelite and Judean kings also explicitly instituted changes in religious practices that served military needs. For example, the HB/OT describes how the Judean king Hezekiah, who inherited the throne from his father around 727, undertook a religious reform that closed all outlying sanctuaries and decreed that all sacrificial rituals must take place at the central sanctuary in the capital city of Jerusalem.[100] He evidently destroyed local religious shrines, reorganized the priesthood and Jerusalem temple, and held a Passover festival to which he invited remnants of the destroyed northern kingdom. When seen in the historical context of Judah's conflicts with Assyria between 714 and 701, it is likely that these actions had political effects if not motives. Such a reform consolidated power in the capital, drew in potential assistance from the old northern kingdom, and centralized economic resources to prepare for a siege of the city. The actions readied Judah for revolt against Assyria near the end of the 8th century.

Alongside these changes that were instituted by the Israelites and Judeans themselves, the majority of war's effects on religion resulted from the influence of both friendly and hostile foreign powers. Cooperative alliances in particular may have been responsible for introducing the worship of other gods into Israel and Judah, since the making of treaties evidently involved tacit recognition and perhaps outright sponsorship of the chief gods of one's allies. The biblical story of King Ahab of Israel, for example, who had an alliance with Phoenicia through his marriage to Jezebel, describes official Israelite sponsorship of the worship of the Phoenician god Baal in the 9th century.[101] Various Assyrian texts also suggest that the making of virtually every kind of political treaty involved worship ceremonies in which each treaty partner honored the other's gods and swore the treaty in the name of both sets of deities.

The submission of Israel and Judah to hostile foreign powers is also likely to have caused changes to their religious beliefs and practices. While the Assyrians did not force their religion on vassal kingdoms, the experience of suffering defeat at their hands

was probably interpreted by some as a sign of the supremacy of Assyria's gods. Moreover, as the influence of foreign kingdoms became increasingly powerful in Israel and Judah, much of the population seemingly absorbed and imitated their religious practices. This mixing of cultures may explain the biblical description of King Manasseh of Judah, who reigned during the peak of Assyria's power in the 7th century and is said to have sponsored Judean worship of "all the host of heaven":

For he rebuilt the high places that his father Hezekiah had destroyed; he erected altars for Baal, made a sacred pole, as King Ahab of Israel had done, worshiped all the host of heaven, and served them.[102]

Certainly when the Assyrians destroyed the northern kingdom in 720 and resettled foreigners into the territory, these settlers brought their own religious traditions, as well as the influence of official Assyrian religion, into Israelite territory.

While the wars of the 9th to the 6th centuries saw some aspects of Israelite and Judean religion become co-opted by the royal establishment or influenced by foreign elements, other groups within the kingdoms, often those outside the centers of power, used religious traditions to challenge the social and political developments. It is possible, for example, that royal land consolidation, cash cropping, and exploitation of peasants generated some of the social legislation in the "Torah" section of the HB/OT (Genesis–Deuteronomy). Several of the biblical law codes presented there as coming directly from Yahweh command fair treatment of the poor, defenseless, and vulnerable in society, and picture Yahweh as most closely tied to those groups:

You shall not withhold the wages of poor and needy laborers, whether other Israelites or aliens who reside in your land in one of your towns. You shall pay them their wages daily before sunset, because they are poor and their livelihood depends on them; otherwise they might cry to the LORD against you, and you would incur guilt.[103]

These laws may have come from other groups of priests or religious figures outside the royal court and may have functioned as an alternative perspective to the monarchy's royal theology.

Prophets

Religious figures called "prophets" represented one reaction to the new social and political developments. The HB/OT has preserved stories about and speeches associated with several of the major prophets. Although commonly thought of as predictors of the future, prophets in ancient Israel and Judah, as elsewhere throughout the Ancient Near East, were more accurately spokespersons or orators who offered a message from Yahweh into particular political and social situations, a message that was not limited to issues of religious belief. Many of these individuals publicly argued against unjust political, social, and economic relations in the name of Yahweh.

The prophets often spoke explicitly about politics and advocated particular courses of action they believed Yahweh wanted the rulers of Israel and Judah to take. The prophet Jeremiah, for instance, was a religious leader in Judah who confronted the kings Jehoiakim and Zedekiah about their foreign policy during the years of 605 to 586 and advocated loyalty to Babylonia in the face of a rising tide of rebellion coming from Egypt. The biblical prophets' speeches also contain specific references to the emerging practices of royal land consolidation and social exploitation of peasant farmers. While the prophets themselves do not appear to have been peasants and did not advocate the establishment of an egalitarian society, they proclaimed that the new socio-economic structures violated the God-ordained historic ethos of Israel as a covenant community, an ethos expressed in Israel's Torah. This ethos meant, according to the prophets, that

Yahweh desired social and economic practices characterized by mutual obligations and just relations among the different levels in the Israelite community.

These convictions led the prophets to condemn Israel's ruling officials and wealthy elites as standing under divine judgment. The prophet Amos, who preached to the people of the northern kingdom in the mid-8th century, proclaimed,

Hear this, you that trample on the needy, and bring to ruin the poor of the land ... buying the poor for silver and the needy for a pair of sandals, and selling the sweepings of the wheat.[104]

The prophet Micah spoke a similar message to the 8th-century leaders of the southern kingdom:

Listen you heads of Jacob and rulers of the house of Israel! Should you not know justice? – you who hate the good and love the evil, who tear the skin off my people, and the flesh off their bones.[105]

Beyond these condemnations of officials, however, the prophets came to see Israel's and Judah's involvement in various conflicts, as well as the unjust consequences that emerged from those conflicts, as acts that would bring divine judgment upon the entirety of both kingdoms. This judgment would take the form of destruction and exile. Thus, according to the prophet Ezekiel, a religious leader taken into exile to Babylonia after 597, Yahweh commanded him,

(A)nd say to the people of the land, Thus says the Lord GOD concerning the inhabitants of Jerusalem in the land of Israel: They shall eat their bread with fearfulness, and drink their water in dismay, because their land shall be stripped of all it contains, on account of the violence of all those who live in it.[106]

Whatever future the prophets envisioned for Israel and Judah rested only upon how Yahweh might redeem them from their violence and restore them after their destruction.

Three faces of Israel and Judah

The history of ancient Israel and Judah has left us with a unique resource for learning about individual civilians from the past. While written records from kingdoms like Assyria and Babylonia preserve the names of individuals, even recording some of their significant deeds and characteristics, these persons are often royal or military officials and any ideas about their personalities, attitudes, or motivations must be hypothesized from usually impersonal annals. For Israel and Judah, however, the Bible is a collection of texts that preserves a large amount of character portraits and personal stories of individual civilians. Many biblical stories are intimate engagements with individuals, frequently claiming to describe their actual words, emotions, and thoughts. In many ways, the HB/OT reads like a collection of in-depth character biographies of people who range from royal to peasant, native to foreigner, and Yahwistic to non-Yahwistic.

This observation does not negate the difficulties associated with using scripture as a historical source. The biblical texts are heavily one-sided in their coverage; for example, the number of male characters vastly supersedes the number of female characters. Many, if not the majority, of the stories were also written long after the times of the persons they describe, in some instances perhaps as many as 500 years later. One cannot simply assume that the biblical portraits of individuals, as intimate and detailed as they may be, are always comprehensive and accurate. Some of the characters may be fictitious, and the Bible depicts all characters, even the ones who are also mentioned in more contemporary, non-biblical sources, by using literary artistry associated with storytelling. Nonetheless, while allowing for creativity and embellishment, for many of the civilians described, there is little reason to doubt that

they, or someone very much like them, experienced life in ancient Israel. At the very least, even if some of the figures have been created by later writers, the historical realities that they are said to experience often match what one would expect for the times in which they are set.

Naboth the vineyard owner

Naboth was the owner of a vineyard in Jezreel, the former capital of the northern Kingdom of Israel. The main story about him appears in 1 Kings 21,[107] and he apparently lived during the reign of King Ahab of Israel in the 9th century (868–853), although it is possible his story belongs to the time of the following dynasty. In any case, Naboth's experiences as a landowner represented well the local impact of the royal policies of land consolidation, power grabbing, and economic control that increased in these years due to trade alliances and military development.

In keeping with the typical family-based socio-economic structures of his day, Naboth possessed a piece of farming land that was his family's inheritance. He may have been simply a local landowner without any significant status, or he may have been one of the "elders" and "nobles" who sat in political and judicial authority in Jezreel – the biblical account can imply either.[108] It seems more likely that he was a wealthy landowner of a large estate, rather than a peasant farmer, and he may have even received a land grant from the crown at some earlier point. Thus, Naboth probably possessed a plot of land on which several peasant farmers worked each day.

What brought Naboth into the memory of history was that his vineyard was next to King Ahab's winter palace in Jezreel. At some point during his reign, Ahab offered to buy

Naboth's vineyard in order to turn it into a royal vegetable garden. The king offered to give Naboth a better vineyard or to pay him the market value of the property. Yet Naboth refused to sell because the land was his family's ancestral inheritance. He appealed to the traditional Israelite ethos that land must remain in the family. Several biblical laws stipulated that the family land could only be transferred through inheritance and that if economic hardship required that the land be sold, it automatically returned to its previous owners at the end of 50 years:

And you shall hallow the fiftieth year and you shall proclaim liberty throughout the land to all its inhabitants. It shall be a jubilee for you: you shall return, every one of you, to your property and every one of you to your family.[109]

Upon his refusal, Naboth fell victim to the ruling dynasty's increasing imposition of control. Ahab's queen, Jezebel, determined to help her dejected husband acquire the land and assert the royal authority that she believed he deserved, orchestrated a conspiracy in which two hired witnesses falsely accused Naboth of blasphemy against God and treason against the king, two crimes punishable by death according to biblical law.[110] On the strength of the legally-required two witnesses,[111] Naboth was executed by stoning: "The two scoundrels came in ... saying, 'Naboth cursed God and the King.' So they took him outside the city, and stoned him to death."[112] After Naboth's execution, Ahab took possession of the vineyard, since apparently all of Naboth's sons were killed as well.[113] But God sent the prophet Elijah to announce a punishment upon Ahab and his dynastic line.

The experiences of Naboth of Jezreel became known to history as a cautionary tale. Although he attempted to resist the royal land consolidation under way in the 9th century, Naboth's life ultimately showed how even wealthy land owners could have their rights violated by the crown. His life represented a protest against these unjust practices, a protest that proclaimed divine judgment on those who perpetrated such injustice.

Small female figurines from the 9th to 7th centuries, such as these, have been discovered throughout the territories of Israel and Judah, and may represent the presence of goddess worship in local and household settings. (akg-images/Erich Lessing)

Huldah the prophetess

Huldah lived in the capital city Jerusalem
during the reign of King Josiah of Judah
(641–610) and was one of the few female
religious figures to be recorded in the
HB/OT. Her main story, which is found
in 2 Kings 22,[114] describes her as "the
prophetess Huldah the wife of Shallum
son of Tikvah, son of Harhas, keeper of the
wardrobe."[115] Depending on whether her
husband worked with the "wardrobe" of the
king or of the priests, Huldah was married
to a member of either the court officials or
temple personnel. She herself was apparently
a court "prophetess." It is unclear precisely
what role such female prophets played in
ancient Israel, although the HB/OT names
four other prophetesses, and texts from
Mari and Assyria testify to female prophets
in those cultures. They probably had
similar functions to male prophets,
which included serving as intermediaries
between the divine and human realms,
and communicating messages from God
concerning specific situations.

The moment of notoriety for Huldah came
in the 18th year of King Josiah (622). At this
time, during a repair project on the Jerusalem
temple, the high priest Hilkiah found what
he called "the book of the law" in the temple:
"The high priest Hilkiah said to Shaphan the
secretary, 'I have found the book of the law
in the house of the LORD'."[116] Scholars have
often concluded that this was an early form of
the biblical book of Deuteronomy, particularly
the section of various blessings and curses
that will come upon the people for obedience
or disobedience to Yahweh. When the book
was read to Josiah, he went into mourning
and ordered the high priest to make an
inquiry of Yahweh concerning the fate
of the king and people.

The high priest Hilkiah, along with the
royal secretary, Shaphan, and three others,
took the book to Huldah. Her role was not to
authenticate the book, since Josiah evidently
accepted its authenticity, but to interpret the
meaning of its contents for the king and
people. In a two-part oracle,[117] Huldah

proclaimed that Yahweh would judge Judah
for its disobedience by bringing destruction
upon the land but Josiah, because he was
repentant, would die before he had to
witness the destruction first-hand:

> ...my wrath will be kindled against this place,
> and it will not be quenched. But as to the King of
> Judah ... because your heart was penitent ... you
> shall be gathered to your grave in peace.[118]

In response to Huldah's proclamation,
Josiah enacted a widespread religious reform in
Judah that called the people into a covenant
of obedience to Yahweh's commands and
centralized worship in the Jerusalem temple.

Baruch the scribe

Baruch the son of Neriah worked as a
"scribe" (Hebrew, *sopher*) in Jerusalem during
the final three decades of Judah's existence
(c.608–586). The book of Jeremiah recorded
his profession and indicated that he was a
close companion of the prophet Jeremiah,
perhaps even serving as his personal
secretary.[119] A *bulla* – an impression in clay
made by a stone seal used to secure the strings
around a letter – that has been recovered from
ancient Judah attests to his profession and
contains the words, "belonging to Berechiah
[an alternate form of the name Baruch], son
of Neriah, the scribe." References in another
biblical text and recovered bulla also suggest
that Baruch came from a family of scribes
and that his brother was the "quartermaster"
under King Zedekiah.[120]

As an ancient scribe, Baruch was a member
of a professional guild that functioned within
the bureaucracy and fulfilled tasks of writing
and record keeping. Since probably only a
small percentage of the Judean population
was literate, scribes served to record events,
note transactions in the temple, and compose
official correspondence. Such writing was
primarily done on clay, potsherds, papyrus,
or leather, and practices from other cultures
indicate that scribes often trained in schools
run by the temple or royal palace.

A representation of Ishtar, the Mesopotamian goddess of war. The goddess appears here with her foot on a lion and next to a worshipper in audience. The worship of Ishtar probably provided some of Assyria's religious motivations for its military undertakings. (Werner Forman Archive)

In this capacity, Baruch served the prophet Jeremiah during the tumultuous years of Judah's rebellions against Babylonia under kings Jehoiakim and Zedekiah (c.605–586). Baruch apparently played a major role in preserving Jeremiah's preaching and forming the biblical book that bears his name. Some biblical scholars even think that Baruch was Jeremiah's biographer and was responsible for most of the book's narratives. Indeed, the reactions of some Judeans to Baruch preserved in the book suggest that he was no mere recorder but actively shaped the political advocacy of the prophet, an advocacy that argued it was Yahweh's will for Judah to surrender to Babylonia: "but Baruch son of Neriah is inciting you [Jeremiah] against us, to hand us over to the Chaldeans, in order that they may kill us or take us into exile in Babylon."[121]

According to Jeremiah 36, around the year 605 as Babylon was establishing its dominance in Syria-Palestine, Jeremiah dictated a scroll of his preaching to Baruch and sent him to read it to a gathering of people during a fast at the Jerusalem temple. An official who overheard the reading then brought Baruch before all the royal officials of King Jehoiakim, and Baruch read the scroll to them. Apparently disturbed by its proclamations of divine judgment, the officials sent the scroll to be read to the king, who subsequently burned the scroll and ordered that Jeremiah and Baruch be arrested for treason. Warned in advance to flee, Jeremiah and Baruch escaped capture, and Jeremiah dictated a replacement scroll to Baruch along with additional materials.

By the time of the Babylonian siege of Jerusalem under King Zedekiah (c.588), however, Jeremiah and probably Baruch with him had been imprisoned in Jerusalem. When the Babylonian siege was temporarily lifted, Baruch went with Jeremiah outside Jerusalem to serve as a legal witness to the prophet's purchase of a piece of ancestral land in Anathoth, a purchase presented as a sign of hope for the eventual restoration of Judah.[122] When Jerusalem finally fell to the Babylonians, Baruch and Jeremiah were released from prison and allowed to remain in the land. But a few years later, when the Babylonian-appointed ruler of Judah was

assassinated, Baruch and Jeremiah went to
Egypt, perhaps being taken by force against
their will, with a group of Judean officials
who feared Babylonian reprisals for the
assassination: "...everyone whom
Nebuzaradan the captain of the guard
had left with Gedeliah ... also the prophet
Jeremiah and Baruch son of Neriah ... came
into the land of Egypt..."[123] Baruch settled in
a town in the northeastern delta, where he
apparently ended his career. In this setting,
although the episode may have occurred
earlier,[124] the book of Jeremiah tells of a
personal prophecy of comfort that Baruch
received from Jeremiah.[125] Baruch, apparently
disheartened by his lack of significance or
effectiveness in his career, received a promise
that Yahweh would preserve his life in the
midst of war and destruction, a gift that

A relief from the southwest palace in Nineveh that
shows two Assyrian scribes recording the spoils of war.
One scribe holds a hinged, wooden tablet, and the other
a papyrus scroll. (Ronald Sheridan/Ancient Art and
Architecture Collection Ltd)

positioned Baruch to carry on the prophet's
message and to symbolize the possibility
of hope for his devastated people.

Baruch became a major figure in later
Jewish literary tradition. Three writings
not included in the Jewish and Protestant
canons of the HB/OT bear his name,
even though they were evidently written
centuries after his death by later Jewish
authors and do not exist in Hebrew.[126] The
development of this later tradition suggests
that Baruch came to be seen as a symbol
of loyalty and obedience in the midst
of a time of unfaithfulness and rebellion.

Judah as a Babylonian province

A series of military conflicts that spanned more than two and a half centuries is unlikely to have a clear conclusion, and the end of Judah's major wars likewise consisted of several developments that unfolded after the Babylonian destruction of Jerusalem in 586. When the city fell at the close of a prolonged siege in mid-July, the Babylonians put into effect the new policy that they had adopted in response to a growing Egyptian threat in the late 590s. This policy entailed making drastic changes in the government of rebellious kingdoms. The Babylonians immediately executed the Davidic king Zedekiah, as well as most of the royal officials, top priests, and local leaders, and took many inhabitants into exile to Babylonia.[127] It appears that the Babylonians allocated about one month to accomplish the exiling of people from Jerusalem and the gathering of the city's spoil, since approximately a month after Jerusalem's capture a Babylonian contingent arrived to raze the city and leave it desolate. Thus, Jerusalem in late 586 was a nearly deserted town, with dismantled walls, destroyed political and religious buildings, and burnt houses.

In the period following these events, several developments brought the history of Judah's major military conflicts to an end: the Babylonians reorganized the government of Judah with a new capital; that new organization collapsed shortly thereafter; and the Babylonians and Judeans reacted to that collapse in various ways. Within this sequence of events, three things appear certain:

1) the Babylonians subjugated Judah, removed the Davidic family from power, and eliminated the historic capital city;
2) Gedeliah son of Ahikam, a Judean royal official not from the ruling Davidic family, was appointed by Babylonia to rule over a depleted Judah from a new center in Mizpah;
3) Gedeliah was subsequently assassinated and his government collapsed.

Beyond these general happenings, the biblical and extra-biblical evidence allows some more detailed speculation.

First, at the time when the Babylonians destroyed Jerusalem and some other major Judean cities in the summer of 586, they treated subjugated territories differently than their predecessors had. While the Assyrians had likewise restructured governmental systems, they had also practiced the physical and economic rebuilding of conquered territories. The Babylonian practice, on the other hand, was to conduct no military operations other than war and to leave conquered territories devastated and impoverished with only relatively minor governmental structures in a particular chosen area. Babylonia's goal appears to have been the establishment of a buffer zone of dilapidated areas between itself and Egypt. Hence, when the former center of the kingdom at Jerusalem collapsed, peripheral areas of the kingdom like the Negev, Jordan Valley, and Shephelah also fell into decline.

In light of these practices, the Babylonian destruction should not be seen as total, and Judah should not be thought of as an "empty land." Although the Babylonians deported many Judean people, removed the ruling dynasty, and left destroyed areas in ruins, the majority of the population seemingly remained in the territory. Archeological evidence shows that most of the devastated areas were southwest of Jerusalem in places like Beth-shemesh and Lachish, and the area immediately north of Jerusalem remained virtually unscathed and even experienced growth during this time. In fact, it is likely that the Babylonians chose this limited area

A modern threshing floor. Such facilities helped produce the grain needed for subsistence, supply, and trade. (Image courtesy of www.HolyLandPhotos.org)

for leniency even before the destruction of Jerusalem. Probably while the siege was underway, they established a new administrative center for Judah at Mizpah in the territory of Benjamin just north of Jerusalem. At this location, the Babylonians stationed a garrison of troops (apparently small enough to be later liquidated by a contingent of only ten men; see below), gathered the major elements of the remaining population, and established a submissive government.

Although the biblical story of the people who remained in the land, which is told in 2 Kings 25 and Jeremiah 40–41, has a noticeable slant in favor of those deported to Babylonia and describes those remaining as only the poorest of the land, there are other indications that they also included priests, scribes, soldiers, officers, artisans, and workers. The exact number of people remaining is unknown, but they probably gathered in the region of Mizpah from the devastated areas. The biblical texts

also indicate that refugees who had fled to neighboring kingdoms like Edom, Moab, and Ammon returned to the new center at Mizpah, as did the remnants of the Judean army commanders:

> *Now when all the captains of the forces and their men heard that the king of Babylon had appointed Gedeliah as governor, they came with their men to Gedeliah at Mizpah...*"[128]

These were probably junior officers of several small army units. Thus, in the aftermath of Jerusalem's destruction, the Babylonians reorganized Judah into a territory centered in Mizpah and extending mainly to surrounding cities like Gibeon and Bethlehem. Archeological remains indicate a population of 400 to 500 people in Mizpah, as well as the emergence of village settlements in some areas throughout Judah. Evidence from burial caves suggests that there may also have been some limited reoccupation of parts of Jerusalem.

In order to administrate the remaining territory, the biblical texts record that the Babylonians appointed Gedeliah ruler over

Judah. Gedeliah was apparently from a socially prominent Judean family, since his grandfather was Shaphan, the royal secretary under King Josiah.[129] He may also have been one of the high-ranking officials within the Judean court of Zedekiah before 586. A bulla discovered at Lachish before its destruction identifies someone named Gedeliah as having been "over the household," a phrase that designated the chief minister of the royal court. Thus, it appears that the Babylonians appointed one of the chief officials who was not from the Davidic ruling family to govern the reorganized territory.

The exact nature of Gedeliah's position remains unclear, however, since the biblical texts do not specify his office. Although most modern Bible translations insert the title "governor" and assume that the Babylonians annexed Judah into a directly controlled province immediately after Jerusalem's fall, there are some indications that Gedeliah may have been installed as a new king and Judah left as a greatly reduced vassal kingdom. Some references in Jeremiah 40–41, as well as a seal found at Mizpah, mention "the king" in the period following Jerusalem's destruction and in connection with people whom the HB/OT lists as being among Gedeliah's officers.

If the Babylonians appointed Gedeliah as a king, rather than a governor, the new Babylonian policy toward rebellious kingdoms probably did not entail immediately turning them into provinces. Rather, the Babylonians may have allowed kingdoms like Judah to remain vassal kingdoms, but with a new ruling family and capital city and in a reduced condition. The dearth of Babylonian records does not permit certainty, and the policy could have taken different forms with regard to different kingdoms. Yet the Babylonians were perhaps following the former Assyrian practice of not provincializing the kingdoms of southern Syria-Palestine that were closest to the Egyptian border. In any case, the biblical texts attribute to Gedeliah the authority to promise Babylonian protection, distribute

A seal discovered at Lachish inscribed with the words, "belonging to Gedeliah, who is over the house," perhaps indicating that Gedeliah was a royal official before being appointed by the Babylonians as ruler of Judah after 586 BC. (Wellcome Library, London)

lands and houses, oversee subsistence resources, and perhaps even collect taxes:

As for me, I am staying at Mizpah to represent you before the Chaldeans who come to us; but as for you, gather wine and summer fruits and oil, and store them in your vessels, and live in the towns that you have taken over.[130]

Even if the Babylonians allowed Judah to persist as a vassal kingdom after Jerusalem's destruction, they annexed it as an imperial province shortly thereafter. The apparent catalyst for this development was the assassination of Gedeliah and the collapse of his administration at Mizpah. The HB/OT

The Babylonian Empire 6th century BC

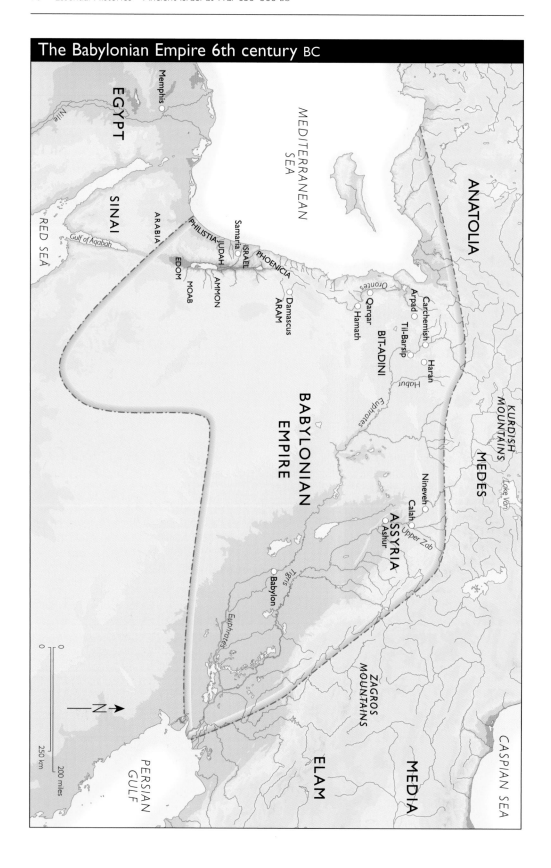

A Judean seal found at Mizpah containing the Hebrew inscription "belonging to Jaazaniah, servant of the king." Jaazaniah was an official under Gedeliah at Mizpah after 586 BC (2 Kgs 25: 23). Because the seal refers to the "king," it may indicate that Gedeliah ruled as king, rather than governor, of Judah after the Babylonian destruction. (©2004 Credit: Topham Picturepoint/Topfoto.co.uk)

describes how some of the Judean soldiers that gathered to Gedeliah at Mizpah had warned him that King Baalis of Ammon had employed Ishmael son of Nethaniah to assassinate him.[131] The biblical texts describe Ishmael as "one of the chief officers of the king," and imply, if the "king" here is Gedeliah, that Ishmael initially submitted to Gedeliah's authority.[132] But the texts also emphasize that Ishmael was "of the royal family," probably indicating that he was a member of the extended Davidic family, although not a son of the previous king Zedekiah.[133] Ishmael no doubt represented opposition to a non-Davidic ruler in Judah and a desire to reinstate the old ruling family.

Ishmael, with a contingent of ten men, eventually succeeded in assassinating Gedeliah and his officers in Mizpah, as well as taking captives, destroying the small Babylonian garrison, and even massacring 80 mourners on their way to the ruins of Jerusalem:

But in the seventh month, Ishmael son of Nethaniah son of Elishama, of the royal family,
came with ten men; they struck down Gedeliah so that he died, along with the Judeans and Chaldeans who were with him at Mizpah.[134]

After the assassination, the soldiers loyal to Gedeliah pursued Ishmael to Gibeon and rescued the captives, but Ishmael escaped to Ammon. Even so, the army officers from Mizpah took the people they had rescued from Ishmael, as well as Jeremiah the prophet, Baruch the scribe, and perhaps others, and fled to Egypt because they feared Babylonian reprisals for the civil unrest in Judah.

The precise date of these climactic events remains uncertain. The biblical texts place them in "the seventh month," but do not provide the year.[135] While the structure of the biblical narrative implies that the assassination happened in 586 shortly after Jerusalem's destruction, it more likely occurred in 582/581, after Gedeliah had ruled for about five years. At this time, the Jewish historian Josephus reports that King Nebuchadrezzar of Babylon campaigned again in Syria-Palestine, a campaign particularly aimed at Moab and Ammon:

And so it happened; for in the fifth year after the sacking of Jerusalem, which was the twenty-third year of the reign of Nebuchadnezzar [582/581 BC], Nebuchadnezzar marched against Coele-Syria and, after occupying it, made war both on the Moabites and the Ammanites.[136]

Jeremiah 52: 30 also records another deportation of 745 Judeans by the Babylonians in this year: "in the twenty-third year of Nebuchadrezzar, Nebuzaradan the captain of the guard took into exile of the Judeans seven hundred and forty-five persons."[137] These references suggest that the Babylonians took punitive action in response to the assassination of Gedeliah and the overthrow of his administration, and that this action occurred in 582/581. While the Babylonians may have allowed Judah to remain a vassal kingdom after 586, it was probably in 582/581 that they finally reduced the kingdom to a province. Judah likely became a part of the Babylonian province that included the territory of the old northern Kingdom of Israel and was governed from Samaria.

At the end of this concluding sequence of events, the various deportations in 597, 586, and 582/581 had probably sent about 20,000 Judeans to Babylonia, but had also left a collection of citizens living in the depleted territory of the former kingdom. Hence, at the end of this period, the people of the kingdom formerly known as Judah existed in different communities in separate locations: those remaining in the land of Judah; those living together in Babylonia; and those who had fled in smaller groups to surrounding kingdoms like Egypt. Throughout the following decades, these groups faced the tasks of forging identities for themselves in the midst of their new situations, and answering the question of where and with whom their future lay.

Forging identities (586–539 BC)

The two and a half centuries of war that ended in 586 BC produced new life situations for the peoples who had previously called themselves "Israelites" and "Judeans", and pushed those peoples to think intentionally about their present and future existence. More specifically, the Babylonian destruction of Jerusalem was a cultural and theological trauma for the people of Judah with consequences on several levels. For example, the HB/OT as a whole indicates that Judeans had long found their sense of who they were through an association with the so-called "promised land" and Jerusalem temple. Obviously, these trends had to be reformulated after the destruction in 586.

The fall of Judah and the subsequent deportations were traumatic on another level because they gave rise to diverse communities of "Judeans" living throughout the Ancient Near East. The HB/OT, especially books like 2 Kings, 2 Chronicles, Jeremiah, and Ezekiel, presents the destruction of Jerusalem in 586 as inaugurating a 47-year "Babylonian exile" (586–539) in which the "true" community of the Judean people lived in Babylonia while awaiting divine restoration to their homeland. While it is true that at least after the collapse of Gedeliah's government in Mizpah by 582/581, the "Judeans" no longer dwelt together in their ancestral land and many found themselves in Babylonia, significant portions of Judah's people continued to live in their ancestral territory while some settled in places like Egypt.

Thus, at least two major communities of people, descended from the inhabitants of the Judean Kingdom, emerged in the decades after 586: those who remained in the land of Judah (now a Babylonian province centered at Mizpah), and those who lived in Babylonia as a result of the deportations of 597, 586, and 582/581. Naturally, these communities tried to forge identities for themselves and envision their futures, drawing on their memories and ideas of the heyday of Judean power in the "promised land." This process produced competing visions that led to an ideological rift between the two communities. Eventually, however, the two communities would encounter one another again when the Persians destroyed the Babylonian Empire and began to send the Judean "exiles" home in 539.

Judeans remaining in the land

The biblical sources relevant to this period were produced or at least edited by the deported community living in Babylonia and thus, like all written sources, represent a particular perspective. Hence, the biblical picture draws a sharp distinction between conditions before and after 586 and implies that there was a nearly complete exile, that the center of cultural and religious life shifted to Babylonia, and that only a meager population of poor people remained in the land of Judah. Especially the latest materials added to biblical texts[138] minimize the number and status of those remaining in Judah, and seem to deliberately conceal their presence there throughout 586 to 539. This perspective, of course, helped to back up the exiles' claim that they were the true community of Judah. Only in this biblical perspective, however, can these years be seen as a time when Judah lived in exile. Archeological remains demonstrate that a community continuous with the preceding culture persisted in the old territory of Judah. Judah was not an empty land during the so-called Babylonian exile. In fact, the majority of Judeans probably remained in

Judah after 586 BC and into the late Babylonian and early Persian periods

the land, perhaps as much as 75 percent of the earlier population.

Because the focus of the relevant biblical texts is elsewhere, very little is known about the community that remained in the land. This community was likely constituted differently than the pre-destruction society. Since deportation had removed much of the upper and artisan classes, there was apparently redistribution of property and resources to the benefit of the lower classes: "Nebuzaradan the captain of the guard left in the land of Judah some of the poor people who owned nothing, and gave them vineyards and fields at the same time."[139] Although the inhabitants in this community officially shifted from being Judean citizens to being Babylonian citizens, they retained an administrative center at Mizpah, and seemingly continued the characteristic elements of their previous lifestyle. Even in the time immediately after Jerusalem's destruction, for example, Gedeliah had instructed the remaining community to resume their normal life and agriculture under Babylonian rule.[140]

In the aftermath of the deportations and destructions, however, the people remaining in the land sought to forge an identity for themselves that could explain their past, present, and future. Advantageous in this regard was the fact that the Babylonians, unlike the Assyrians, did not resettle foreigners into conquered territories but practiced only one-way deportation to Babylonia. Thus, the people in Judah did not meld into a society of blended ethnic groups as the population of the northern Kingdom of Israel did after its destruction in 720. The fact that Judah was, then, still populated by Judeans allowed the continuation of the worship of Yahweh to become a key element in the construction and maintenance of the community's identity. Although the HB/OT gives the impression that all cultic activity stopped in Judah after the destruction of the temple, several specific texts suggest that Yahweh worship of some kind persisted at various locations. The Babylonians may have established Mizpah to function as a combined administrative and religious center, in much the same way that Jerusalem had functioned previously. Additionally, some people apparently continued to worship at the ruins of the Jerusalem temple. The book of Lamentations, for example, assumes that cultic rituals were taking place at the destroyed temple. Such worship was probably informal, characterized by mourning and repentance, and carried out through meal and incense offerings rather than animal sacrifices.

This continued cultic activity forged community identity in particular ways. Mourning and repentance rituals served to help the people explain and cope with the catastrophic events that had befallen their kingdom. Yet such activities specifically created a vision of identity that saw those taken to Babylonia as the sinners who had incurred divine judgment and thus brought about the kingdom's destruction. Note how the prophet Ezekiel, himself one of the exiles, says the community in the land labeled the deportees as those who "have gone far from the LORD."[141]

Judeans in Babylonia

Only a few biblical and extra-biblical sources provide details of the lives of the Judeans deported to Babylonia between 597 and 582/581. In the HB/OT, the primary sources are the book of Ezekiel, a prophet who was taken into exile in 597 and carried out his preaching among the deportees in Babylonia, and Isaiah 40–55, the words of a prophet who lived in exile near the end of the Babylonian Empire (c.539). The deportees probably totaled in the tens of thousands and were primarily settled in the depleted area between Assyria and Babylonia that had been devastated during wars between the two empires. Note that many of the names of the Judean settlements contain the word "Tel" ("mound") and thus imply that the deportees were mainly moved into areas in need of redevelopment (e.g. Tel-Abib[142]). While some Judeans undoubtedly assimilated into Babylonian culture in these contexts, the Babylonians, unlike the Assyrians before them, did not force ethnic intermingling. In fact, Babylonian policy apparently was to settle deportees in groups according to their origins and ethnicity and allow them some limited self-governance. For example, the biblical texts record the use of ethnic titles like "the elders of Judah" and the "elders among the exiles" to designate leaders among the deportees.[143]

The Judean exiles received different treatment depending on their social status, but certainly were not slaves. Kings like Jehoiachin, the Judean king when Jerusalem fell in 597, were imprisoned, but Babylonian records note that he and his sons received grain rations and that he was later released from prison and given a place in the royal court.[144] Non-royal deportees were likewise not oppressed or restricted in significant ways, since Babylonian texts contain the names of Judeans who were involved in commercial, real-estate, and economic activities like normal Babylonian citizens. Overall, the exiles served as something like land-tenants to the Babylonian king, who provided needed labor, tax revenues, and military service.

Even so, the cultural and theological disorientation of being displaced from their homeland left the exiles needing to forge a social and religious identity that could account for their present and envision their future. As with those remaining in Judah, the continuation of Yahweh worship in Babylonia formed part of this effort. Since the Jerusalem temple had been the stipulated place for animal sacrifices, Judeans in exile apparently had a non-sacrificial religion that focused on gatherings of prayer, praise, and perhaps the reading of Torah in local meeting places. Such gatherings may have been the early forerunners of Jewish synagogues, though the synagogues' full realization seems to have developed later in the Roman period. Along the same lines, the religious practices of Sabbath observance and circumcision became important designators of ethnic identity, as witnessed by the

biblical books of Ezra and Nehemiah that come from the exile community.

The continued presence of members of the Davidic royal line among the exiles in Babylonia also furthered a sense of religious and national identity and fostered hope for future restoration. Biblical texts produced during this period, for example, continued to number the years in exile as part of King Jehoiachin's reign.[145] The survival of descendants from this family throughout the time of the Babylonian Empire also helped to confirm in the audience's minds prophetic proclamations that an "anointed one" ("Messiah") would emerge as a future Davidic leader and bring about the restoration of the exiles: "I will make them one nation in the land, on the mountains of Israel; and one king shall be king over them all... My servant David shall be king over them."[146] Thus, the Judean community in Babylonia constructed a competing vision of identity to that of the community that remained in the land. Prophets like Ezekiel proclaimed that Yahweh had abandoned the land of Judah and accompanied the exiles to Babylonia and that they represented the true community that Yahweh planned to restore to the homeland.[147] A bright future awaited the "good figs" that had been sent into exile, but a bleak future was in store for the "bad figs" that remained in the land of Judah:

Thus says the LORD, the God of Israel: Like these good figs, so I will regard as good the exiles from Judah... I will set my eyes upon them for good, and I will bring them back to this land.[148]

The major tool by which the Judean community in Babylonia forged its social and religious identity was the production and editing of written texts that have now become part of the Jewish and Christian scriptures. The HB/OT itself reveals that there was widespread literary activity among the community in Babylonia. In fact, the majority of the texts that now appear in the HB/OT were either written or given their final edited form by this exilic community in order to serve their effort to construct an identity. For example, exilic editors collected the speeches of prophets like Hosea, Isaiah, and Jeremiah, recontextualized and expanded their words in light of the new situation, and shaped them into the literary compilations that eventually became today's biblical books. In the hands of the exilic community, these prophetic texts served to reinterpret the destruction and deportation as simply the first part of Yahweh's plan to make Israel and Judah a faithful people, a plan that also included a return to the promised land after a period of cleansing.[149] The prophetic messages proclaimed that the destruction and exile did not represent the weakness or failure of Judah's God but were carried out on his orders. Prophets like Jeremiah even recast Nebuchadrezzar of Babylon as the "servant" whom Yahweh used to enact his plan:

Now I have given all these lands into the hand of King Nebuchadnezzar of Babylon, my servant, and I have given him even the wild animals of the field to serve him.[150]

Some of the biblical texts composed or compiled among the exiles emphasized the possibility of living a faithful and prosperous life by submitting to Babylonian authority as divinely ordained. Biblical stories like those of Joseph,[151] Daniel, and Esther, characters presented as living in the capitals of foreign empires, probably began to take shape during this period and held up their heroes as models of a faithful lifestyle in the courts of foreign kings. This emphasis again underscored the conviction that deportation was not an end in itself but was part of a divine plan moving toward restoration.

The most significant example of scripture's role in shaping the exilic community's sense of identity is the so-called "Deuteronomistic History," which includes the biblical books of Joshua, Judges, 1 and 2 Samuel, and 1 and 2 Kings, and may have originated as a unified work. These books offer an extensive narrative presentation of Israelite and Judean history from its beginning to the middle of the exile.

While an earlier version of this work may have been written before 586, the present form underwent significant expansion and editing during the time of the exilic community. These books are, of course, selective in their reporting and often allow religious concerns to shape their presentation. Rather than being deficiencies, these characteristics suggest that the Deuteronomistic History was composed not simply to report but to interpret the events that resulted in the destructions and deportations of the 6th century. On the whole, the work answers the questions of what happened and what will happen in terms of religious faithfulness. Israel's and Judah's fate depended upon faithfulness to their God, but their unfaithfulness generated divine punishment. This interpretation again allowed the exilic community to see their present circumstances as part of Yahweh's plan and generated hope that renewed faithfulness would lead to a good life in the present and restoration in the future. Hence, 2 Kings 25 concludes the Deuteronomistic History with the report of King Jehoiachin's release from prison in Babylon and achievement of an exalted seat in the Babylonian court:

In the thirty-seventh year of the exile of King Jehoiachin of Judah ... King Evil-merodach of Babylon, in the year that he began to reign, released King Jehoiachin of Judah from prison; he spoke kindly to him, and gave him a seat above the other seats of the kings who were with him in Babylon.[152]

Return, rebuilding, and resistance

The two major Judean communities that emerged after 586 came into contact with one another again when the Babylonian Empire gave way to the new world power of Persia around 539. After the death of Nebuchadrezzar, there was a rapid succession of relatively unsuccessful Babylonian kings that reached a climax with Nabonidus, a ruler who emerged from a western part of the Empire outside the capital (555–539). This ruler alienated much of the population through religious reforms and spent a decade away from the capital, leaving his son ruling as a regent. During these years of Babylonian decline, the Persians, an Indo-European people centered in the area of modern Iran, rose to power under Cyrus II. Babylonian records indicate that Cyrus began as a lesser ally of Nabonidus, but eventually captured the city of Babylon without a fight in October 539. This event inaugurated the so-called "Persian period" or "Achaemenid period" that lasted until the ascendancy of Alexander the Great of Greece around 333.

The historical sources for the entire Persian period, especially for events concerning Judah, are very limited, and the main sources are biblical writings like 1 and 2 Chronicles, Ezra, Nehemiah, Haggai, and Zechariah. Virtually all of these sources focus exclusively on the deportees rather than on the community that remained in the land. What the available biblical and Persian texts suggest, however, is that the Persians adopted a different policy of empire

The "Cyrus Cylinder" contains a cuneiform inscription in which King Cyrus of Persia permits a deported people to return to their homeland. Although it does not mention Judeans, it suggests that the allowance of such returns was Persian policy in the late 6th century. A similar decree appears for the Jews in Ezra 1: 1–4 and 6: 3–5. (c) The British Museum/HIP/Topfoto.co.uk)

building: they allowed deportees to return home and rebuild their local temples and capitals, a move likely designed to refortify distant areas of the Empire. For example, the "Cyrus Cylinder" is a piece of Persian propaganda that seemingly testifies to the policy of sponsoring the rebuilding of local religious sites:

> ... I returned (the images of) the gods to the sacred centers [on the other side of] the Tigris whose sanctuaries had been abandoned for a long time, and I let them dwell in eternal abodes. I gathered all their inhabitants and returned (to them) their dwellings.[153]

Probably as a result of this policy, the Judeans living in Babylonia received the opportunity to return to Jerusalem and rebuild its temple. The HB/OT preserves different versions (in both Hebrew and Aramaic) of an "Edict of Cyrus" that inaugurated these events:

> Thus says King Cyrus of Persia: The LORD, the God of heaven, has given me all the kingdoms of the earth, and he has charged me to build him a house at Jerusalem in Judah. Any of those among you who are of his people – may their God be with them! – are now permitted to go up to Jerusalem in Judah, and rebuild the house of the LORD, the God of Israel – he is the God who is in Jerusalem.[154]

The mound of remains that marks the site of ancient Lachish, the major fortified city in southwestern Judah in both the Assyrian and Babylonian periods. The Assyrians commemorated the city's destruction in 701 BC with a pictorial relief on the wall of Sennacherib's palace in Nineveh (see book cover). (R Sheridan, Ancient Art and Architecture Collection)

The biblical texts, dedicated to the interests of the deportees, give the impression of a massive, all-at-once, return from Babylonia in the early Persian period, and supply lists of names that imply the return of about 50,000 people under the leadership of a Persian-appointed governor named Sheshbazzar.[155] The names of the officials in these lists, however, are from later years and suggest that the lists may reflect periods after 539. There are, in fact, diverse traditions preserved in the Bible about how the process of return occurred and under whose leadership. Both the Cyrus Cylinder and the Edict of Cyrus imply that the original return was specifically connected with those who would rebuild the temple and thus was probably very limited. Most likely, the return of Judeans from Babylonia was a gradual process that occurred in several waves over nearly a century, perhaps beginning with an initial return of about 4,000 people in the early 530s. The combined biblical traditions suggest at least four phases of return:

1) an initial return under Sheshbazzar in 538;
2) a movement that completed the rebuilding of the temple under the Persian-appointed governor Zerubbabel and the high priest Joshua around 515;
3) a return concerned with religious reform led by the priest Ezra in 458;
4) an effort aimed at refortifying Jerusalem's walls led by the governor Nehemiah in 445.

The significance of these developments rests in the situation they created within the land of Judah, a situation that represented the resolution of the effects of centuries of war and shaped the land's future well beyond the 6th century. After 539, the former Kingdom of Judah existed as a Persian province called "Yehud," with its religious and economic center in Jerusalem. Yehud was part of the larger imperial district called "Abar Nahara" ("across the river"), which included most areas west of the Euphrates. The province of Yehud itself consisted primarily of the area from just above Bethel to just below Beth-zur and from the Jordan River to just west of Azekah, an area about 25 miles (40km) north–south and 30 miles (48km) east–west. Persia took an active role in the administration of this province, often appointing its political and religious leaders (e.g., Ezra and Nehemiah). Although the refortification of Jerusalem's walls around 445 returned that city to its status as the center of the area, it remained a smaller version of its former self with a population of probably no more than about 500 people throughout the first century of Persian rule. Not until the 2nd century BC would Jerusalem again achieve a significant population.

Perhaps more significantly, the return of some deported Judeans created a situation of internal conflict in Yehud between the returnees and those who had remained in the land. The HB/OT attests to opposition from locals to the rebuilding of Jerusalem and its temple: "Then the people of the land discouraged the people of Judah, and made them afraid to build."[156] One cause of such conflict may have been that while the Babylonians apparently appointed governors from locals in the province, the Persians sent members of the Davidic line back from Babylonia and reestablished the rule of the Judean elite. Hence, a new

ruling class of priests associated with the Jerusalem temple emerged and disenfranchised those local political and religious leaders. This situation of external provincialization and internal conflict would characterize Yehud's existence from the time of the rebuilding of the temple and city walls until the rise of the Greek Empire (c.515–333). During this time, Yehud simply existed as one of many provinces in the Persian Empire and virtually disappeared from historical view amidst the conflicts among powers like Persia and Egypt.

Also important for understanding the consequences of Israel's and Judah's many centuries of war is the fact that the province of Yehud after the rebuilding did not comprise the sole location of the former inhabitants of the Kingdom of Judah. Only from the Bible's perspective can we say that the "exile" ended. The centuries of war throughout the Assyrian and Babylonian periods ultimately concluded with pockets of former Judean citizens, now rightly called "Jews," living in dispersed places like Yehud, Babylon, Egypt, and elsewhere. Thus, the legacy of the kingdoms of Israel and Judah was not a restored kingdom with set borders, but rather diverse communities living in various geographical and political contexts, people somewhat united by ethnicity and shared religious practices. This constitution would give shape to the Jews' participation in the subsequent eras of world history.

Further reading

Ahituv, S. and E. Oren, eds, *The Origin of Early Israel – Current Debate: Biblical, Historical, and Archaeological Perspectives*, Ben Gurion University of the Negev Press, Beer-Sheva (1998)

Ahlstrom, G., *The History of Ancient Palestine*, Fortress, Minneapolis, (1993)

Albertz, R., *Israel in Exile: The History and Literature of the Sixth Century B.C.E.*, Society of Biblical Literature Press, Atlanta (2003)

Anglim, S. *et al.*, *Fighting Techniques of the Ancient World, 3000 BC–AD 500, Equipment, Combat Skills and Tactics*, Thomas Dunne Books, New York (2002)

Arnold, B., *Who Were the Babylonians?*, Society of Biblical Literature Press, Atlanta (2004)

Aubin, H., *The Rescue of Jerusalem: The Alliance between Hebrews and Africans in 701 BC*, SOHO, New York (2002)

Barnes, W.H., *Studies in the Chronology of the Divided Monarchy of Israel*, Scholars Press, Atlanta (1991)

Becking, B., *The Fall of Samaria*, Brill, Leiden (1992)

Borowski, O., *Daily Life in Biblical Times*, Society of Biblical Literature Press, Atlanta (2003)

Brettler, M., *The Creation of History in Ancient Israel*, Routledge, London (1995)

Bright, J., *A History of Israel*, Westminster John Knox, Louisville (2000)

Chapman, C., *The Gendered Language of Warfare in the Israelite-Assyrian Encounter*, Eisenbrauns, Winona Lake (2004)

Chavalas, M., and K.L. Younger, eds, *Mesopotamia and the Bible: Comparative Explorations*, Baker Academic, Grand Rapids (2002)

Cline, E., *Jerusalem Besieged: From Ancient Canaan to Modern Israel*, University of Michigan Press, Ann Arbor (2004)

Cogan, M., *Imperialism and Religion: Assyria, Israel and Judah in the Eighth and Seventh Centuries B.C.E.*, Scholars Press, Missoula (1974)

Cogan, M., ed., *The Oxford History of the Biblical World*, Oxford University Press, Oxford (1998)

Davies, P., *In Search of 'Ancient Israel'*, JSOT Press, Sheffield (1992)

Dawson, D., *The First Armies*, Cassell, London (2001)

Day, J., *In Search of Pre-Exilic Israel*, T&T Clark, London (2004)

De Odorico, M., *The Use of Numbers and Quantifications in the Assyrian Royal Inscriptions*, University of Helsinki Press, Helsinki (1995)

Dever, W., *What Did the Biblical Writers Know and When Did They Know It? What Archaeology Can Tell Us About the Reality of Ancient Israel*, Eerdmans, Grand Rapids (2001)

Finkelstein, I. and N. Silberman, *The Bible Unearthed: Archaeology's New Vision of Ancient Israel and the Origin of Its Sacred Texts*, Free Press, New York (2000)

Finkelstein, I. and N. Silberman, *David and Solomon: In Search of the Bible's Sacred Kings and the Roots of the Western Tradition*, Free Press, New York (2006)

Frame, G., *From the Upper Sea to the Lower Sea: Studies on the History of Assyria and Babylonia in Honour of A.K. Grayson*, Nederlands Instituut voor het Nabije Oosten, Leiden (2004)

Freedman, D.N., ed., *The Anchor Bible Dictionary*, Doubleday, New York (1992)

Fretheim, T., *Deuteronomistic History*, Abingdon, Nashville (1983)

Gabriel, R., *The Military History of Ancient Israel*, Praeger, Westport (2003)

Gale, R., *Great Battles of Biblical History*, The John Day Co., New York (1970)

Galil, G., *The Chronology of the Kings of Israel and Judah*, Brill, Leiden (1996)

Gallagher, W., *Sennacherib's Campaign to Judah*, Brill, Leiden (1999)

Grabbe, L., ed., *Can a "History of Israel" be Written?*, Sheffield Academic Press, Sheffield (1997)

Guild, N., *The Assyrian*, Scribner, New York (1987)

Hallo, W. and K.L. Younger, eds, *The Context of Scripture*, Brill, Leiden (1997–2002)

Hayes, J.H. and P.K. Hooker, *A New Chronology for the Kings of Israel and Judah and Its Implications for Biblical History and Literature*, John Knox, Atlanta (1988)

Hayes, J.H. and J.M. Miller, eds, *Israelite and Judaean History*, Westminster, Philadelphia (1977)

Herzog, C. and M. Gishon, *Battles of the Bible: A Modern Military Evaluation of the Old Testament*, Random House, New York (1978)

Hobbs, T.R., *A Time for War: A Study of Warfare in the Old Testament*, Michael Glazier, Wilmington, Delaware (1989)

Hoerth, A., G. Mattingly, and E. Yamauchi, eds, *Peoples of the Old Testament World*, Baker, Grand Rapids (1994)

Hughes, J., *The Secrets of the Times: Myth and History of Biblical Chronology*, JSOT Press, Sheffield (1990)

Irvine, S., *Isaiah, Ahaz, and the Syro-Ephraimitic Crisis*, Scholars Press, Atlanta (1990)

Ishida, T., *History and Historical Writing in Ancient Israel: Studies in Biblical Historiography*, Brill, Leiden, (1999)

Keefe, A., *Woman's Body and the Social Body in Hosea*, Sheffield Academic Press, Sheffield (2001)

Kelle, B.E., *Hosea 2: Metaphor and Rhetoric in Historical Perspective*, Society of Biblical Literature Press, Atlanta (2005)

Kelle, B.E. and M.B. Moore, eds, *Israel's Prophets and Israel's Past: Essays on the Relationship of Prophetic Texts and Israelite History in Honor of John H. Hayes*, T&T Clark, London (2006)

King, P. and L. Stager, *Life in Biblical Israel*, Westminster John Knox, Louisville (2001)

Kitchen, K., *The Third Intermediate Period in Egypt (1100–650 B.C.)*, Aris and Phillips, Warminster (1986)

Kitchen, K., *On the Reliability of the Old Testament*, Eerdmans, Grand Rapids (2003)

Knoppers, G. and J.G. McConville, eds, *Reconsidering Israel and Judah: Recent Studies on the Deuteronomistic History*, Eisenbrauns, Winona Lake (2000)

Kofoed, J.B., *Text and History: Historiography and the Study of the Biblical Text*, Eisenbrauns, Winona Lake (2005)

Kuan, J.K., *Neo-Assyrian Historical Inscriptions and Syria-Palestine*, Alliance Bible Seminary Press, Hong Kong (1995)

Lipinski, E., *The Aramaeans: Their History, Culture, and Religion*, Peeters, Leuven (2000)

Lipschits, O., *The Fall and Rise of Jerusalem: Jerusalem under Babylonian Rule*, Eisenbrauns, Winona Lake (2004)

Lipschits, O. and J. Blenkinsopp, eds, *Judah and the Judeans in the Neo-Babylonian Period*, Eisenbrauns, Winona Lake (2003)

Lipschits, O. and M. Oeming, eds, *Judah and the Judeans in the Persian Period*, Eisenbrauns, Winona Lake (2006)

Liver, J., ed., *The Military History of the Land of Israel in Biblical Times*, Israel Defense Force Publishing House, Jerusalem (1964)

Long, V.P., ed., *Israel's Past in Present Research: Essays on Ancient Israelite Historiography*, Eisenbrauns, Winona Lake (1999)

Matthews, V., *A Brief History of Ancient Israel*, Westminster John Knox, Louisville, (2002)

Matthews, V. and D. Benjamin, *Social World of Ancient Israel 1250–587 B.C.E.*, Hendrickson, Peabody (1993)

McDermott, J., *What Are They Saying about the Formation of Israel?*, Paulist, New York, (1988)

McKay, J., *Religion in Judah under the Assyrians 732–609 B.C.*, A.R. Allenson, London (1973)

Miller, J.M. and J.H. Hayes, *A History of Ancient Israel and Judah*, Westminster, Philadelphia (1986)

Miller, P.D., *The Religion of Ancient Israel,* Westminster John Knox, Louisville (2000)

Moore, M.B., *Philosophy and Practice in Writing a History of Ancient Israel,* T&T Clark, London (2006)

Nelson, R., *The Historical Books,* Abingdon, Nashville (1998)

Noth, M., *The Deuteronomistic History,* University of Sheffield Press, Sheffield (2001)

Olmstead, A.T., *History of Assyria,* University of Chicago Press, Chicago (1960)

Oppenheim, L., *Ancient Mesopotamia: Portrait of a Dead Civilization,* University of Chicago Press, Chicago (1977)

Organ, B., *Is the Bible Fact or Fiction? An Introduction to Biblical Historiography,* Paulist, New York (2004)

Person, R., *The Deuteronomic School: History, Social Setting, and Literature,* Brill, Atlanta (2002)

Pitard, W., *Ancient Damascus: A Historical Study of the Syrian City-State from the Earliest Times until its Fall to the Assyrians in 732 B.C.E.,* Eisenbrauns, Winona Lake (1987)

Provan, I., V.P. Long, and T. Longman, *A Biblical History of Israel,* Westminster John Knox, Louisville (2003)

Rainey, A., *The Sacred Bridge: Carta's Atlas of the Biblical World,* Carta, Jerusalem (2006)

Redford, D., *Egypt, Canaan, and Israel in Ancient Times,* Princeton University Press, Princeton (1992)

Saggs, H.W.F., *The Might That Was Assyria,* Sidgwick and Jackson, London (1984)

Sasson, J., ed., *Civilizations of the Ancient Near East,* Hendrickson, Peabody (2000)

Tetley, M.C., *The Reconstructed Chronology of the Divided Kingdom,* Eisenbrauns, Winona Lake (2004)

Thiele, E., *The Mysterious Numbers of the Hebrew Kings,* Zondervan, Grand Rapids (1983)

Ussishkin, D., *The Conquest of Lachish by Sennacherib,* Tel Aviv University Institute of Archaeology, Tel Aviv (1982)

Van de Mieroop, M., *A History of the Ancient Near East c. 3000–323 B.C.,* Blackwell, Oxford (2003)

Van der Woude, A.S., ed., *The World of the Old Testament,* Eerdmans, Grand Rapids (1989)

Vaughn, A., *Theology, History, and Archaeology in the Chronicler's Account of Hezekiah,* Scholars Press, Atlanta (1999)

Vaughn, A. and A. Killebrew, eds, *Jerusalem in Bible and Archaeology,* Society of Biblical Literature Press, Atlanta (2003)

Von Soden, W., *The Ancient Orient: An Introduction to the Study of the Ancient Near East,* Eerdmans, Grand Rapids (1994)

Yadin, Y., *The Art of Warfare in Biblical Lands in the Light of Archaeological Study,* McGraw-Hill, New York (1963)

Yamada, S., *The Construction of the Assyrian Empire: A Historical Study of the Inscriptions of Shalmaneser III (859–824 BCE) Relating to his Campaigns to the West,* Brill, Leiden (2000)

Endnotes

1   see 2 Kgs. 15: 11; 16: 19
2   2 Kgs. 16: 2; New Revised Standard Version (NRSV)
3   2 Kgs. 16: 1; NRSV
4   1 Sam. 14: 47; 1 Kgs. 11: 23–25
5   see 1 Kgs. 14: 25–27
6   1 Kgs. 4: 20–21
7   compare Josh. 1–12 and Judg. 1–2
8   see 1 Kgs. 9: 15–19
9   see Judg. 7: 16–22
10   1 Kgs. 4: 26; 9: 19; NRSV
11   2 Kgs. 1: 9–13
12   1 Kgs. 22: 34
13   1 Kgs. 22: 47–49
14   2 Kgs. 9: 25; 15: 25
15   1 Kgs. 16: 9; 2 Kgs. 9: 5
16   2 Chr. 26: 13; NRSV
17   *Context of Scripture* 2.119B: 303
18   *Context of Scripture* 2.117C: 288
19   see 1 Kgs. 22
20   *Ancient Near Eastern Texts Relating to the Old Testament,* 560
21   see 1 Kgs. 16: 15–2 Kgs. 8: 27; 2 Chr. 17–20
22   see also 1 Kgs. 16: 24
23   1 Kgs. 16: 31; NRSV
24   *Context of Scripture* 2.23: 137
25   2 Kgs. 3: 4
26   1 Kgs. 22: 47
27   1 Kgs. 15: 20; NRSV
28   *Context of Scripture* 2.39: 161
29   cf. 2 Kgs. 8: 18 and 8: 26
30   1 Kgs. 22: 4
31   1 Kgs. 22: 44
32   1 Kgs. 20; 22
33   *Context of Scripture* 2.113A: 263
34   2 Kgs. 8: 18
35   *Context of Scripture* 2.113A: 264
36   2 Kgs. 1: 1; 8: 20; NRSV
37   2 Kgs. 3; cf. 2 Chr. 20
38   2 Kgs. 3: 9, 16, 20; NRSV
39   2 Kgs. 9–10
40   *Context of Scripture* 2.113F: 270
41   2 Kgs. 10; 13
42   2 Kgs. 13: 3; NRSV; see also 10: 32–33; 12: 17–18
43   2 Kgs. 14
44   2 Kgs. 14: 25; NRSV; see also 14: 28
45   see Amos 1: 3–5
46   see Amos 1–2
47   2 Kgs. 15: 37
48   2 Kgs. 15: 19; NRSV
49   2 Kgs. 15: 25
50   Isa. 7: 1, 7; NRSV; cf. 2 Kgs. 16; 2 Chr. 28
51   2 Chr. 28: 7
52   2 Kgs. 15: 29
53   *Context of Scripture* 2.117A: 286
54   *Context of Scripture* 2.117G: 292
55   Hos. 1: 10–11; 2 Kgs. 17: 2
56   2 Kgs. 17: 3
57   2 Kgs. 17: 4a
58   2 Kgs. 17: 4a
59   2 Kgs. 17: 4b
60   2 Kgs. 17: 5–6; 18: 10
61   Hos. 8: 4; author's translation
62   *Context of Scripture* 2.118A: 293
63   *Context of Scripture* 2.118E: 296; cf. 2 Kgs. 17: 6, 24
64   Isa. 20–22
65   2 Kgs. 18; 2 Chr. 29
66   NRSV
67   2 Kgs. 18: 14; NRSV
68   see 2 Kgs. 18: 17–19: 7
69   cf. Isa. 36
70   2 Kgs. 18: 29–30, 33, 35; NRSV
71   *Context of Scripture* 2.119B: 303
72   see 2 Kgs. 22–23
73   cf. 2 Kgs. 23 and 2 Chr. 35
74   see Jer. 47: 1
75   2 Kgs. 24: 2; NRSV
76   2 Kgs. 24: 6; 2 Chr. 36: 6
77   *Ancient Near Eastern Texts Related to the Old Testament,* 564
78   Jer. 27: 1–3
79   Jer. 51: 59

80   2 Kgs. 25: 1, 3; NRSV
81   2 Kgs. 25: 7; NRSV
82   2 Kgs. 25; Jer. 52
83   see 1 Kgs. 22: 34
84   2 Kgs. 15: 27
85   2 Kgs. 15: 37; NRSV
86   see 2 Kgs. 15: 25
87   e.g., 2 Kgs. 7: 2, 17, 19
88   e.g., Exod. 15: 4; 1 Kgs. 9: 22;
      Ezek 23: 15, 23
89   see Judg. 9: 54; 1 Sam. 14: 1–17;
      2 Sam. 18: 15
90   2 Kgs. 15: 25; NRSV
91   2 Kgs. 16: 5; NRSV; cf. Isa. 7: 1
92   2 Chr. 28: 6; NRSV
93   Hos. 2: 2; 5: 13; NRSV
94   *Context of Scripture* 2.117C: 288
95   2 Kgs. 15: 30; NRSV
96   Exod. 15: 3, 6; NRSV
97   Deut. 1: 30; 3: 22; NRSV;
      see also Deut. 33; Judg. 5
98   Ps. 2: 5–6, 7–8; NRSV;
      see also Ps. 18; 110
99   see Lev. 2; 6; 7
100   see 2 Kgs. 18; 2 Chr. 29–31
101   1 Kgs. 16
102   2 Kgs. 21: 3; NRSV
103   Deut. 24: 14–15; NRSV; cf. Exod. 22:
      21–24; Deut. 10: 17–18; 15: 7–11
104   Amos 4: 4, 6; NRSV
105   Mic. 3: 1–2; NRSV
106   Ezek. 12: 19; NRSV
107   see also 2 Kgs. 9: 21–26
108   see 1 Kgs. 21: 8
109   Lev. 25: 10; NRSV
110   Exod. 22: 28; Lev. 24: 14–16
111   Deut. 17: 6; 19: 15
112   1 Kgs. 21: 13; NRSV
113   2 Kgs. 9: 26
114   cf. 2 Chr. 34
115   2 Kgs. 22: 14; NRSV
116   2 Kgs. 22: 8; NRSV
117   2 Kgs. 22: 16–17, 18–20
118   2 Kgs. 22: 17–20; NRSV
119   Jer. 32, 36, 43, 45
120   Jer. 51: 59
121   Jer. 43: 3; NRSV
122   Jer. 32
123   Jer. 43: 6–7; NRSV
124   see Jer. 45: 1
125   Jer. 45
126   Baruch, 2 Baruch, 3 Baruch
127   see 2 Kgs. 25: 11–12
128   2 Kgs. 25: 23; NRSV
129   see 2 Kgs. 22: 8
130   Jer. 40: 10; NRSV; cf. 2 Kgs. 25: 24
131   Jer. 40: 13–16
132   Jer. 41: 1
133   Jer. 41: 1
134   2 Kgs. 25: 25; NRSV;
      cf. Jer. 41: 2–7
135   2 Kgs. 25: 25; Jer. 41: 1
136   *Antiquities* X: 180–182
137   NRSV
138   see, e.g., 2 Kgs. 24–25; Jer. 40
139   Jer. 39: 10; NRSV; cf. 2 kgs. 25: 12
140   see Jer. 40: 9–10
141   Ezek. 11: 14–15
142   see Ezek. 3: 15
143   Jer. 29: 1; Ezek. 8: 1
144   see 2 Kgs. 25: 27–28
145   e.g., Ezek. 1: 2
146   Ezek. 37: 22, 24; NRSV
147   see Ezek. 10–11
148   Jer. 24: 5–6; NRSV
149   see Hos. 1–3; Ezek. 37
150   Jer. 27: 6; NRSV
151   Gen. 37–50
152   2 Kgs. 25: 27–28; NRSV
153   *Context of Scripture* 2.124: 315
154   Ezra 1: 2–3; NRSV; cf. 2 Chr. 36:
      22–23; Ezra 6: 3–5
155   Ezra 2; Neh. 7
156   Ezra 4: 4; NRSV

Index

Visit the Osprey website

- Information about forthcoming books

- Author information

- Read extracts and see sample pages

- Sign up for our free newsletters

- Competitions and prizes

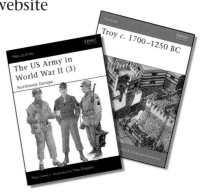

www.ospreypublishing.com